secrets of a
faith well lived

max lucado brennan manning sheila walsh

chonda pierce grant jeffrey patsy clairmont steve brown

barbara johnson henry blackaby larry crabb scotty smith

tony campolo karyn henley frank peretti

secrets of a
faith well lived

intimate conversations
with modern-day disciples

christopher coppernoll

HOWARD
PUBLISHING CO.

Our purpose at Howard Publishing is to:
- *Increase faith* in the hearts of growing Christians
- *Inspire holiness* in the lives of believers
- *Instill hope* in the hearts of struggling people everywhere

Because He's coming again!

Secrets of a Faith Well Lived © 2001 Christopher Coppernoll
All rights reserved. Printed in the United States of America

Published by Howard Publishing Co., Inc.
3117 North 7th Street, West Monroe, Louisiana 71291-2227

01 02 03 04 05 06 07 08 09 10   10 9 8 7 6 5 4 3 2 1

Edited by Michele Buckingham
Interior design by Stephanie Denney
Cover design by LinDee Loveland

Library of Congress Cataloging-in-Publication Data
Coppernoll, Christopher L., 1963-
   Secrets of a faith well lived : intimate conversations with modern-day disciples / Chris
Coppernoll.
      p. cm.
   ISBN 978-1-58229-191-8
   1. Christian life. I Title.

BV4501.3 .C68 2001
277.3'083'0922—dc21   2001024952

Scripture quotations not otherwise marked are from the Holy Bible, New International Version.
Copyright © 1973, 1978, 1984 International Bible Society. Used by permission of Zondervan
Bible Publishers. Other Scripture quotations from The Holy Bible, Authorized King James
Version (KJV), © 1961 by The National Publishing Co.; The Holy Bible, New King James
Version (NKJV), © 1982 by Thomas Nelson, Inc.; New American Standard Bible (NASB), © 1973
by The Lockman Foundation; the Holy Bible, New Living Translation (NLT), © 1996 by
Tyndale House Publishers, Inc.; and The Living Bible (TLB), © 1971 by Tyndale House
Publishers, Inc.

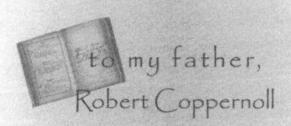

to my father,

Robert Coppernoll

about the author

Christopher Coppernoll is the host of the internationally syndicated weekly radio show *Soul2Soul* and the author of *Soul2Soul: Top Christian Music Artists Share an Intimate Look at Their Lives, Their Music, and Their Faith.* He has conducted more than three hundred interviews with Christian recording artists and authors on living faith in contemporary times. He lives in Franklin, Tennessee, with his wife and daughter.

contents

Acknowledgments

To the transcriptionists who transformed the interview tapes for
Secrets of a Faith Well Lived into written text,
Shelley Bright, Melissa and Paul Sekora,
and my mother, Lois Coppernoll: Thank you for your persistence!

———◆———

To everyone at Howard Publishing Company,
especially Denny and Philis Boultinghouse:
Everyone speaks so highly of Howard Publishing.
I'm delighted to have my own firsthand experience
of working with you. Thank you for publishing my book.

———◆———

To my brilliant editor, Michele Buckingham:
I hope everyone will appreciate what a special contribution
you've made, as I do.

———◆———

To my friends Emily Kohl and Michael Dukes
at Turning Point Media Relations in Nashville, Tennessee:
Thanks for your friendship and your commitment
to the authors and recording artists you represent.

To my publicist and friend, Brian Smith:
Few walk and inspire as do you.

To Robert Wolgemuth, Jennifer Cortez,
and everyone at Wolgemuth and Associates, past and present:
Thanks for your representation on this project.

To the authors interviewed in this book:
You've inspired so many of us with your words
through the years, whether spoken or in print.
Thank you for taking the time from your very busy schedules
to share your faith, your lives, and your stories with all of us.

To my family, Lori and Gray: I love you both very much.

To my Lord, Savior, and Friend, Jesus:
Where few wanderers stop, You've made Yourself a home.

Introduction

What's the Secret?

It has been said that our world is shaped by the stories we tell; and likewise, we as individuals become sculpted by the stories we hear. That's why I believe Christians have a great obligation—a calling, if you will—to open ourselves up in those private zones where each of us live and disclose to others the secrets of our faith. We must be brave enough to engage others with our own faith stories. After all, there's nothing quite as compelling as a personal testimony. The mere act of confiding how God makes Himself real in our lives has power to transform and elevate both the story's teller and its hearer.

I believe in the power and significance of personal testimony. By trade I interview Christian personalities (yes, there is such a job!), and in that role I'm allowed to pose probing questions to those I interview and ask about their personal faith. As host of the internationally syndicated *Soul2Soul* radio program—a show that collects and disseminates faith stories shared primarily by Christian music artists—I've found myself sitting across from Christian artists such as Amy Grant, Michael W. Smith, Jars of Clay, Randy Travis, Jennifer Knapp, Rebecca St. James, Newsboys, and Point of Grace, listening to them describe how God has impacted their lives. Some of these interviews became the basis for my first book, *Soul2Soul*.

In *Secrets of a Faith Well Lived*, I was able to carry out an inspiration I had more than twenty years ago when I imagined taking all of my questions about what it means to be a Christian to an expert who could help me make sense of it all. How great it would be, I reasoned, to sit with someone I trusted and respected—someone who understood by study and personal life experience what it means to be faithful to the call of Christ's discipleship—and ask my questions. I finally got that opportunity—and what an experience it turned out to be! Only I didn't just sit and talk with one expert but fourteen, their names known around the world as some of the most influential Christian authors of our time.

HENRY BLACKABY is director of the Office of Prayer and Spiritual Awakening at the North American Mission Board of the Southern Baptist Convention and is best known for his modern classic, *Experiencing God*. Henry's other books include *Created to Be God's Friend*, *The Man God Uses*, *When God Speaks*, *The Power of the Call*, and *Fresh Encounter: God's Pattern for Revival and Spiritual Awakening*. Henry also serves as special assistant to the president of the International Mission Board and LifeWay Christian Resources, consulting in the area of prayer and spiritual awakening for global revival.

STEVE BROWN served as a pastor for twenty-five years and now works full-time with his radio ministry, *Key Life*. In addition to being a radio broadcaster, he is a popular speaker, a seminary professor, and the author of such books as *Follow the Wind*, *Approaching*

God, How to Talk So People Will Listen, and *When Your Rope Breaks.* Steve serves as professor of preaching at Reformed Theological Seminary in Orlando, Florida, and is on the board of the National Religious Broadcasters. He co-hosted his own television series with Tony Campolo on the Odyssey Network called *Hashing It Out.*

TONY CAMPOLO is the author of twenty-eight books, including such bestsellers as *Following Jesus without Embarrassing God* and *Is Jesus a Republican or a Democrat?* He is a professor of sociology and the chairman of the sociology department at Eastern College in St. Davids, Pennsylvania, and holds a Ph.D. from Temple University. He is also an ordained minister and the associate pastor of Mount Carmel Baptist Church in West Philadelphia. Known for his involvement in social issues, Tony is a frequent guest on such wide-ranging television programs as *Nightline* and *Politically Incorrect.*

PATSY CLAIRMONT is a well-known humorist and best-selling author of such books as *God Uses Cracked Pots, Normal Is Just a Setting on Your Dryer,* and *Stardust on My Pillow,* her first fiction work. Patsy is also a popular speaker at the nationally renowned Women of Faith conferences and has addressed more than one million women around the country. She has written five books cooperatively with the other Women of Faith speakers, including *Joybreaks, We Break for Joy, Joyful Journey,* and *Outrageous Joy.* Her latest book, *Mending Your Heart in a Broken World,* focuses on lessons of healing and grace.

LARRY CRABB, who holds a Ph.D. in clinical psychology from the University of Illinois, is the author of fifteen books, including *Connecting, Inside Out, The Silence of Adam, The Marriage Builder,* and *The Safest Place on Earth.* He is a professor and Distinguished

Scholar in Residence at Colorado Christian University, where he was chairman of the Master of Arts in Biblical Counseling Program from 1989 to 1996. Larry is much in demand as a conference and seminar speaker and as a Bible teacher.

KARYN HENLEY is an award-winning author and children's communicator. She is best known as the author of *The Beginners Bible*, which has sold more than three million copies and been translated into seventeen languages. She also authored *God's Story*, a chronological Bible for young readers. A graduate of Abilene Christian University, Karyn has created numerous resources to equip parents to nurture the faith of their children. She was recently named one of the "Top 10 People Who Have Changed the Face of Children's Ministry during the 1990s" by *Children's Ministry Magazine*.

GRANT JEFFREY is the founder of Frontier Research, a popular conference speaker, and the best-selling author of numerous books dealing with Jesus, prophecy, and the trustworthiness of Scripture. His books include *Jesus: The Great Debate, Journey into Eternity, The Handwriting of God*, and *The Signature of God*, the latter two dealing with the mysterious and controversial "Bible codes." With Angela Hunt, he also has written two fiction thrillers, *Flee the Darkness* and *By Dawn's Early Light*.

BARBARA JOHNSON is a humorist and the best-selling author of such books as *Living Somewhere between Estrogen and Death, He's Gonna Toot and I'm Gonna Scoot, Leaking Laffs: Between Pampers and Depends, Stick a Geranium in Your Hat and Be Happy, Splashes of Joy in the Cesspools of Life*, and *Where Does a Mother Go to Resign*. She is the founder of Spatula Ministries, an organization that ministers to hurting parents. Barbara is also one of the most popular speakers in the country, speaking to more than 350,000 women each year at Women of Faith conferences and in other settings.

MAX LUCADO, pulpit minister of Oak Hills Church of Christ in San Antonio, Texas, has more than sixteen million books in print. He is the author of such favorites as *He Chose the Nails, Just Like Jesus, Six Hours One Friday, No Wonder They Call Him the Savior, In the Grip of Grace, When God Whispers Your Name, He Still Moves Stones,* and *The Applause of Heaven.* In 1997 Max set a new publishing industry record by placing seven different titles concurrently on the hardcover bestsellers list of the Christian Booksellers Association.

BRENNAN MANNING is a former Franciscan priest and the author of such works as *The Ragamuffin Gospel, Abba's Child,* and *Ruthless Trust: The Way of the Ragamuffin.* As a member of the Little Brothers of Jesus of Charles de Foucauld, he embraced a stoic lifestyle that included manual labor, silence, and prayer. He also accepted assignments as a mason's assistant, shoveling mud and straw in Spain; and as a voluntary prisoner in a Swiss jail, where his identity as a priest was known only to the warden. Brennan eventually left the Franciscan order and married. He works today as an author and speaker.

FRANK PERETTI, with more than nine million books in print, has been called America's most popular Christian novelist. His best-selling books include *This Present Darkness, Piercing the Darkness, The Visitation,* and *Prophet.* His novel *The Oath* sold more than half a million copies within the first six months after its release and was awarded the 1996 Gold Medallion Award for best fiction. Frank also wrote The Cooper Kids Adventure Series, which has become the best-selling children's series of all time.

CHONDA PIERCE, best known as a comedian, has also authored several books, including *It's Always Darkest before the Fun Comes Up* and *Second Row, Piano Side!* Her videos, *Having a Girls' Nite Out, On Her Soapbox,* and *Four-Eyed Blonde,* are among the best-selling Christian comedy videos ever. Chonda is a frequent speaker with the Women of Faith conferences and has performed at Billy Graham crusades. She's also had a part in Bill Gaither's Homecoming video series. Recently Chonda added "vocalist" to her list of accomplishments when she recorded her first musical album, *Yes & Amen.*

SCOTTY SMITH is the senior pastor of Christ Community Church in Franklin, Tennessee, and the author of three books: *Unveiled Hope* with recording artist Michael Card, *Speechless* with Steven Curtis Chapman, and *Objects of His Affection* about the relentless love of God. A graduate of Westminster Theological Seminary in Philadelphia, Scotty has been influential within the Christian music community in Nashville as both mentor and friend to many Christian recording artists. He contributes a weekly audio message, "Sixty Seconds with Pastor Scotty Smith," to the internationally syndicated radio program *Soul2Soul.*

SHEILA WALSH, former co-host of the *700 Club,* is well-known as a Women of Faith conference speaker. She is the best-selling author of such books as *Honestly, Living Fearlessly, Life Is Tough but God Is Faithful,* and *Stories from the River of Mercy.* Sheila is also a talented singer/songwriter whose albums include *Love Falls Down—Songs of Worship, Hope, Future Eyes, Blue Waters,* and *War of Love,* which earned her both Grammy and Dove award nominations and the International Artist of the Year Award from the Gospel Music Association.

———

Collectively, the writings of these authors over the years have inspired and helped deepen the faith of millions of readers around the globe. However, my intention in this book is not to explore their words and works but rather the writers themselves. Obviously, the fourteen authors I interviewed differ in background, age, gender, and denomination. Their stories distinguish them as individuals with varied life experiences. But they all have this in common: their faithfulness to Christ.

The interviews were conducted during an eighteen-month period between 1998 and 2000. I wanted to know if these successful and respected authors have personal stories yet untold, perhaps written in the margins of their lives. I wanted to hear their own testimonies in their own words. I asked some questions boldly and eagerly, as a student who waves his hand in the air to get the teacher's attention. Others I asked quietly and privately, as one who discreetly approaches a teacher after class. Do they ever have doubts? Have they experienced failure? Do they face challenges common to us all? And has their experience of living in Christ shown them something about Jesus that could be—should be—shared in the telling of their personal stories?

As I asked questions and listened carefully to the answers, I realized that I was observing the faith of spiritual giants. I heard a maturity that comes only from years of following Christ. I witnessed their confidence in God *even in the midst of their own unanswered questions.*

I learned that the books that have inspired us so much were written by *real* people.

I also learned something about my own expectations for perfection this side of heaven. Wise mentors all, the authors shared with me not only their triumphs as Christians but, even more revealing, their disappointments in themselves. Yes, their professional prestige and distinction as people of character spark us to become more like Christ; but it is their admission of failures and shortcomings that is a comfort to those of us who strain for perfection yet continue to fall woefully short.

Some of the interviews stand out for their humor, others for their insight, all for their inspiration. Of course, you may find yourself reading a statement or two you disagree with. That's OK. You will still find much to move you in each author's candid witness of what living the Christian faith really means to him or her.

I think it's significant that these fourteen authors agreed to come together to take part in this book. All of them knew at the time of their interviews that their words would coexist with the words of the others, to be stirred and mixed together into a cohesive whole. The interviews weren't lifted from existing books or magazines, so they carry the pulse and tempo of a synergetic community. And isn't that what the church is—people coming together as a team? In these pages some of our top teacher-players join their voices and share their stories of faith for our spiritual enrichment, comfort, and good. My prayer is that you will discover the faith so dear to these Christian authors. Their own personal journey with God is perhaps the greatest story each will ever tell.

Secret #1

Purpose Means Building Our Lives around God's Plans

The richest men in the world can't buy it, but the poorest can have it for free. Many of the world's most educated scholars can't understand it, yet the simple-minded among us often grasp it with ease. What is it? *Purpose.* Purpose is like a corset holding together the bustle of today, with its hectic pace and problems, and the ideals of tomorrow, with its myriad possibilities and dreams. It is a simple concept, yet it has the capacity to confuse and elude all of us at times. Without it we fritter away our days in the pursuit of things that have about as much value as tumbleweeds. But understanding our purpose is always within our reach—it's as close as our willingness to follow God.

Certainly, each of us wants to enjoy the life we've been given. But along with the blessings of daily living come daily distractions as well. No sooner are we confidently moving in one direction, sure of who we are and what we're doing, than suddenly we're persuaded to change course, last year's good intentions replaced by this year's frenzied day planner. The problem? We've forgotten our purpose—or perhaps we never knew it.

Deep down inside we all want to know two things: Does God love us? And does He have a purpose for our lives? If only He would appear before us and speak unmistakably, we think—like He did for Moses with that eye-catching burning bush—surely *then* we'd know what we're supposed to do with our short time here on earth. But the truth is God rarely works that way. Few of us ever have burning-bush experiences. That doesn't mean that God wants to hide our purpose from us; on the contrary, He wants to reveal our purpose and make it known to us. We simply need to do one thing: ask.

God still speaks to His children. He still answers our cries for help and understanding. His primary dialogue, of course, is in His Word, the Holy Bible, and it pours out the clear and wonderful message of His infinite love and timeless purpose for us all. Then God further reveals His purpose for our individual lives through the Holy Spirit, often speaking in times of prayer and through the wise input of the people around us at home or at church.

Ultimately, the purpose of our lives is best defined by the Westminster Shorter Catechism: "Man's chief end is to glorify God, and to enjoy Him forever." To glorify God means to bestow honor upon Him, to worship Him, to praise Him. And we do all of these things when we simply *obey Him*. When we obey God the Father, we are automatically in His perfect will for our lives—and that means we have found our chief purpose! To enjoy Him, then, becomes not so much our duty as our reward.

Still, most of us, when we begin to reflect on what God wants us to do with our lives, start by asking the more mundane, practical questions: Where should I live? Whom shall I marry? What kind of career should I pursue? But God's will for our lives isn't wrapped up in the answers to those questions. Rather, finding God's will involves our saying to Him—and to ourselves—that we'll do *whatever He wants us to do*. When we agree to this, we're ipso facto placed on *His* schedule for our lives, not our own. The mind-set of "Whatever You want, Lord" resets our lives to a clean, blank, unhurried slate that God can then write on with His perfect choices for us.

As we give Him that blank slate and place our cares in the hands of the One who cares for us, we find ourselves making different choices than the ones we used to make. We find ourselves doing what He would have us do instead of what we used to do. We begin to do good because He is good. Life becomes exciting and fulfilling—elements that were always just out of reach when we were the ones in charge of ourselves. We have purpose!

Of course, finding our purpose is only the beginning. Walking out that purpose—following our Lord and Savior, Jesus Christ, day by day—is an exciting and joyful adventure. Like a train standing at the station, its doors open wide and its engines powerfully idling, we have only to get on board. Our destination awaits. Jesus wants to personally direct our paths and be our guide, our teacher, and our friend along the way.

Living with purpose is simple, but it's not always easy. In this chapter, the authors I interviewed talk about their own purpose in life. What is it? How did they find it? Do they sometimes still struggle with giving God the reins? Like each of these authors, you and I can know and live out our purpose on this earth. Like them, we can make each moment count for something larger than a moment. We simply need to put ourselves fully in the hands of our loving and purposeful God and say, "Whatever You want, Lord." That way we'll be sure to build our lives around God's plans for us.

Before Frank Peretti was a household name in the world of Christian publishing, before This Present Darkness *became a sensational bestseller, Frank was a struggling writer by night and a factory worker by day. What motivated him to write— and keep writing? Here Frank tells how he found his purpose in life.*

Frank Peretti

I started writing because that's what God made me to do. I've always been very strongly motivated that way. Primarily, it's the creative spark that drives me to write. I think, *OK, I've got this creative spark. Now what am I supposed to do with it?* I made a covenant with myself and with the Lord that it's not enough just to write; I really should be saying something valuable because I've got an overall calling on my life to build up the body of Christ. So my guiding principle is: What can I write to help, to edify, to teach, to build up the body of Christ?

I've got more writing to do. There's no point in my saying, "Yep, I've made it. Think I'll just sit here and enjoy my success for a while." What's the point of that? The Lord put me in this position to write. He gave me a name in the publishing business, and He gave me an audience. Whenever I go out and meet people, they tell me that they've been blessed and touched by my books. They ask, "When are you going to come out with the next one?" So I'm thinking of them. I'm saying, "What do I need to tell them next?"

A pastor or Sunday school teacher does the same thing. There's no difference. Every week a pastor sits down and prayerfully asks, "What can I share with the congregation this Sunday? What can I do to feed and nurture them?" A Sunday school teacher preparing a lesson asks, "What can I say to those kids? How can I build them up in the body of Christ? How can I make them more like Jesus?"

I'm kind of in that place myself. I'm a teacher, an exhorter, and a builder. I'm like them. I don't look upon my ministry and my task as being at the top of some heap somewhere. I look at it and say, "OK, I've finally got a job!" Now I just want to make sure I do it well.

building the kingdom

I'm a builder. That's the simplest way to put it. There are many different callings. There are those who sound warnings; there are those who rebuke. I get all kinds of suggestions for topics people think I should write about. "Frank, you should write a book about the homosexual agenda." "You should write a book about the education system." "You should write a book about the new world order." Just two days ago someone said, "You need to write a book about the rapture." I nearly fell over. As if Tim LaHaye and Jerry Jenkins haven't done enough writing about the rapture!

I was at a Christian conference once—a "prophecy conference" where the speakers addressed such topics as current events in Russia and the Middle East and how they bear upon the unfolding of Bible prophecy. Standing outside the auditorium, I listened to a couple of the speakers as they shared back and forth about all the horrible things that are going on in the world—the plots, the conspiracies, the corruption in government, the various ways our freedoms are being threatened, rampant disease, bacterial warfare, Saddam Hussein, Russian submarines. It struck me: *I don't know a lot about these kinds of things.* I wondered if I should know more.

In that moment the Lord spoke to me. I suddenly realized that it's not my calling to write about all the garbage going on in the world. It's my calling to build, to nurture, to nourish the body of Christ. I could found an entire ministry on ferreting out horrible things and making sure the body of Christ knows all about them. I could know all about the Russians selling missiles and Saddam Hussein working on bacterial weapons. But it occurred to me that I could know all about this stuff, or I could know nothing about it; the outcome would be exactly the same, because there's really nothing I can do about any of it.

the big picture

We need to be putting our energy into the stuff we really can do something about. And in all honesty, the only thing we can do something about is building the body of Christ, building the kingdom of God. This world is passing away. Kingdoms are going to rise, and kingdoms are going to fall. God will have His way, and He will unfold prophecy according to His plan. It is our job to prepare people—to feed, nurture, and build the body of Christ—because that's God's ultimate plan: to redeem a bride for Christ.

As I looked at the big cosmic picture of things, I realized I could write all kinds of books that scare people about the horrible things happening in the world, or I could write books that equip, nourish, and strengthen God's people—that help them to take a stand, to know what they believe, to be encouraged in their Christian walk, and to avoid the pitfalls that can beset us. I want to do the latter, because I believe that's the most worthwhile way for me to spend my time and energy.

———

Often the events and challenges of our lives shape what we do. I asked Women of Faith speaker Barbara Johnson, the best-selling author of such books as Living Somewhere between Estrogen and Death *and* He's Gonna Toot and I'm Gonna Scoot, *why she has made encouraging others her life's work. As Barbara explains, sometimes it's just the credentials.*

Barbara Johnson

People have to listen to me because I've been in the valley. I've been in the pits. I lost two sons, and my third son disappeared for eleven years because I didn't know how to handle something in his life. He disowned us, changed his name, and said he never wanted to see us again. So I have been through a lot, and I have credentials. When I get up and talk, I know what I'm talking about.

I really believe in the ministry of encouragement. The word *encourage* means "to fill the heart." There are a lot of lonely, hurting women out there with empty hearts and broken dreams. When you lose a child, that's a broken dream. When a child becomes estranged, that's a broken dream. I've been through the broken dreams; yet God has taken the fractures in my life, put them back together, and infused me with joy. When I go out and speak to women's groups or write books, I think that underlying joy comes through.

I'm so glad when people come up to me and say, "I read your book, and it changed my life." That change didn't happen because I know anything about literary style. I've never had a class in writing. I didn't write a word until I was fifty years old. Now I have more than three million books in print in twenty-four languages. That's a miracle! God took a fractured piece of my life, a life that was a mess, and put it together so that I can bless other people.

———

When God gets hold of our hearts, we change. With great gusto, honesty, and humor, author and seminary professor Steve Brown tells the story of how his purpose in life changed many years ago. Steve served as a pastor for more than twenty-five years. But by his own account, he started his ministry with goals that weren't meant to go the distance—goals that were eventually replaced by a heart devoted to serving Christ.

Steve Brown

The ministry I'm involved with, Key Life, has a very extensive mission statement. But a simplified version of our purpose is this: "Getting people home—that is, to heaven—with freedom, joy, and faithfulness to Christ as their crowning achievement." We teach about the fact that God isn't angry with us and that the doctrine of Christ's imputed righteousness means we really are free. We try to demonstrate this principle and live it out.

At the beginning of my ministry, however, the goals I had were selfish ones: to have a big church, to be well known, and other things I'm not really proud of. I wish I could say something more spiritual, like I wanted to win the world for Christ or go to the mission field or see my city changed. But I really didn't have those kinds of goals.

I'm not proud of what I was like when I first went into the ministry. I wasn't even a Christian. Of course, we Presbyterians know I became a Christian two thousand years ago. But at least as far as my experience to that point was concerned—and it was quite liberal—I was not red hot for God. The goals that I had at that time were not good goals.

Still I read a book early in my ministry that convinced me it was best to allow my circumstances to determine what I would do in my life. I suppose if you were to take that principle and universalize it, the world would be in serious trouble! But for me, my life's verse has always been from Ecclesiastes: "Whatever your hand finds to do, do it with all your might."

———

As the Holy Spirit leads us, we often find ourselves traveling pathways we never imagined ourselves taking. Following our God-given passion, we wind up surprised by our purpose! Take for example Scotty Smith, the senior pastor at Christ Community Church in Franklin, Tennessee.

Scotty Smith

I was a senior in high school in 1968 when I became a Christian. The parables of the pearl of great price and the treasure in the field became a reality really fast. I had a background of abusing alcohol big time and playing keyboards in a rhythm and blues band. When I discovered the gospel, I was, like, *This is truth!*

getting the call

I remember feeling some sense of vocational call to ministry as a freshman in college in the fall of 1968, although I didn't use that language at the time. I simply felt a call to ministry. I remember sitting in a church and hearing almost audibly two words in the form of a question spoken in my soul. The question was, *Why not?* I knew what that meant: Why not invest as much of my life as possible communicating that which I had found to be true?

I had been planning on going into pharmacy for some reason. I don't know why. I hate chemistry. No one in my family is a pharmacist. But I shifted from pre-pharmacy, and I said, "OK, God is calling me to some form of ministry, but I know it will not involve going to seminary or working in an institutional church." My stereotype was that seminary is really a cemetery; it's where people go to lose their love for Christ.

The Lord has a way of making us eat our words. I wanted to give my heart, my life, my body, my being to the study and dissemination of this truth called the gospel. I had all of these images of how I would do this, but the Lord did not give me the big picture. He just gave me the next step. It became obvious in time that God had called me to teach the Scriptures. That's when I realized the Peter Principle—we rise to the level of our incompetence. Clearly, I needed more training. A good friend of mine said, "You should go to seminary."

I'd been shaped by Francis Schaeffer's writings, so I wondered,

"Where did Francis Schaeffer go to seminary?" The answer is Westminster Seminary, and that's where I went. When I got to seminary, I realized that despite my original objections, that was where I was supposed to be.

anything but a pastor

At the time I still was planning on *not* being a pastor. I couldn't think of anything more boring or disgusting than being a pastor. I just wanted to know how to think and communicate the theology of grace. By my last semester I was still clueless about what I was going to do. I assumed I might go to work at one of the L'Abri Fellowships in Europe. But the Lord had other plans. My wife got pregnant during our last semester in seminary, and we moved back to North Carolina. When you are with child, the whole paradigm shifts! I mean, it's one thing for it to be just you and your wife; you've got a lot more freedom to make plans. But when God puts that first arrow in the quiver, new issues emerge!

We decided to spend a season doing youth ministry. I thought, *That's safe. That's not the pastorate.* But in spending time in youth ministry in a local church, the Father helped me to confront my stereotypes and fears concerning the pastorate.

Being a child of the '60s, I had some well-founded as well as some exaggerated stereotypes of what a pastor was. I grew up in a church that did not preach the gospel, and most of my images of the pastorate were of very boring people who were out of touch culturally, theologically, and in every other way. I also had the image that once you get paid for preaching the gospel, the voice of authority you have in the nonbelieving community is diluted and compromised. I thought I'd rather become a very involved layman—a businessman involved in ministry on the side. But that's the way pragmatists think, not the way the Spirit leads us. I had to overcome my stereotypes and my pragmatism. God does indeed call His people into all spheres of life, but it became obvious in time that He had called *me* to be a pastor.

And not just any pastor. That was another thing I had to overcome: I had a one-dimensional view of the pastorate. I didn't know that being a pastor can take many, many forms. I had never been exposed to creative models of pastoring. So when I began to see people who had this calling who were living in ways counter to my stereotypes, I got very excited. I finally felt a release to consider becoming a pastor, to accept that my teaching gifts would be used not primarily in the classroom but in the context of the larger body of Christ. I became a pastor, planted a church, and step by step the Lord led me into the unfolding of His will for my life.

———

Former 700 Club co-host Sheila Walsh is a speaker, an author, and a contemporary recording artist. Since she is multitalented and involved in so many arenas, I asked her what she considers her ministry and purpose to be.

Sheila Walsh

I would say that my ministry is to encourage people to come out of the shadows where they are living and into the light of God. I remember a day when I was going out to a meeting wearing a white suit. My son, Christian, wanted to say good-bye, so he ran up and threw his arms around me. Unfortunately he had been eating a cup-cake, and I ended up covered in chocolate frosting!

I thought, *I never want to forget this moment because that is how we are supposed to come to God.* You don't go tidy yourself up and take a shower and brush your teeth first. You come as you are—with cupcake all over your face and fingers—and throw yourself into His arms, burying your face in the mane of the Lion of Judah. If I am able to encourage people to come out of the shadows and let themselves be seen, known, and embraced by God, then I will feel like I've lived my life well.

Ruth Graham, Dr. Billy Graham's wife, helped me once when she said that most Christians today go to their Christian bookstore and simply read whatever current books are out. I learned from her that we need to go back and delve into the classics. We need to find those footsteps that go back a few hundred years. The more we study—the more we look at the life of someone like Augustine, for example—the more we see that these people struggled with the exact same things we all struggle with in our lives. We are encouraged when we see that the people we look up to as tremendous saints of the church were also flawed human beings like you and me. They made mistakes too. They did not get it all right.

Not one of us will ever get it all right. But the purpose of my life is not to get it all right. The purpose of my life is to fall in love with Jesus and be a conduit of His love for the world, full stop. That is it.

I asked Sheila how she tended to view herself. Was she primarily an author, a speaker, or a recording artist?

My primary love is communication, and that communication comes in many different forms. I love to write, and that is why I think of myself as a writer more than an author. If no one wanted to publish anything I wrote ever again, I would still write. I don't see writing as a way to pass on what I've learned to other people. I write every day because I see it as a way of learning myself. I don't write about things I know; I write about things I want to know *about*. The whole process of writing makes me delve deeper into subjects.

I also don't see myself as a recording artist. I don't want a music career; I don't want to be out touring and doing all that stuff. Those things are wonderful. But I see music as one more arm with which to reach out, grab hold of someone, turn their faith around, and tell them about the love of God.

Music is one of the few things from this planet that we will take with us into eternity. It has a unique way of being able to capture us unaware. Someone stands up in a pulpit and says, "Now I'm going to talk to you about the love of God," and you think, *Yeah, right, buddy. You don't know what kind of week I've had.* But a song is not like that. Someone stands up to sing, and you mentally sit back in your soul and listen. Sometimes God can creep in and touch you with a song in ways you could never imagine.

———

God often raises up visionaries—men and women who have big ideas about what our world could be like. He also raises up crusaders to advance those ideas. Larry Crabb, author of Connecting, Inside Out, *and* The Safest Place on Earth, *shares his vision of Christians living in real community with one another. But as he explains, having the vision isn't enough; he wants to help make it happen.*

Larry Crabb

I think I've been a frustrated crusader all my life. Over the years I've developed certain theories of counseling. I don't look back on them badly; I don't repent of them. I think they've been all right, but I believe my thinking has been so developmental that I've only been flirting on the outskirts of things. I feel like I've been on the back porch of the home, and only now am I finding the door to get inside the living room where the family meets.

Yeah, I want to be a crusader. I think the church is a mess. I think Christian community is a mess. It's a mess partly because we've lost our vision of community. We've lost our vision of relationship.

Real community has got to start with just a couple of people. It's got to start with my wife and me. We've been married for thirty-three years, and we still fight. We still have struggles and tensions, and she gets mad at me and I get mad at her. But there's got to be something inside us that asks, What is possible between a man and a woman in a marriage relationship? What is possible between a father and his son or daughter? What is possible between a couple of buddies?

I do a lot of public speaking, and I talk to audiences of all different sizes. It has been convicting for me to realize that I sometimes feel most comfortable wearing a microphone behind a podium and talking to a thousand people. I speak fairly well, people tell me, and the audience responds. I tell a story; people laugh. I say something poignant; there's a sense of movement. I could live on that feeling and miss the reality of community.

My fear is that a whole lot of pastors do exactly that. In our

Christian celebrity culture, all the celebrities run around the world and speak to huge audiences. We go to listen to them and feel as if we've found the real thing, but we haven't!

The real thing is a couple of folks getting together. Can you imagine two or three people in somebody's home, lying on the floor, weeping before God over the horror of a particular sin, finishing up with the Lord's Supper, and just being thrilled with forgiveness and with their relationship with God and each other? When is the last time a believer has prayed for an hour with another believer, weeping together over sin, weeping for joy, and embracing one another with the wholeness of the gospel? When is the last time *I've* done that? If we haven't done that, we're not the church.

———

We can't help but put ourselves into a great story when we hear it. Henry Blackaby is the director of the Office of Prayer and Spiritual Awakening at the North American Mission Board of the Southern Baptist Convention and best known for his modern classic, Experiencing God. *Here he tells the story of how he found his purpose in life. Inside his story is a lesson for all of us who aspire to find our own.*

Henry Blackaby

My mission is to obey God. Jesus said, "Wherever the master is, that's where the servant needs to be also." I'm not ignorant of what He's asked me to do. He said, "Henry, you just need to open the Scriptures and guide My people to practice in their lives everything I have commanded." That's my assignment: to walk with my Lord and make sure that I'm following Him, that I'm where He wants me to be; and then to share a message with the people He sends me to that focuses on Him and ensures that none of His people miss what He has in mind.

The "heart" reason that I am where I am comes from a life commitment I've made to do whatever God asks. It also comes from my heritage in a significant way. My uncle and his wife were missionaries in Manchuria during the Great Revival in China and worked with Jonathan Goforth in the early 1900s. Their example set in motion in my heart the understanding of what God can do if He has a people who respond to Him.

Later, while my wife and I were pastoring in Saskatoon, Canada, we witnessed what was called the Canadian Revival—a huge movement of God that shook the city of Saskatoon and had an impact around the world. As a pastor my heart cry had been for revival and awakening. Growing up in Canada, seeing that nation with maybe only 6 percent who were born again, knowing that there was no historical record of any mighty move of God—these things gave me a burden for revival there. Revival is the only thing I know of that can turn a nation around. We were in Canada praying for two years before the revival, and we stayed ten years afterward and saw the hand of God.

Out of that background, I was asked to direct the Office of Prayer, Revival, and Spiritual Awakening at the Home Mission Board for the Southern Baptist Convention. That request matched everything I saw God doing in my life as well as a commitment I made to Him six years before. My commitment was that if the convention—which had been so good to us—ever had a need and sensed that we could make a contribution, my answer to their call would be yes. So when they called and said, "You're the only one we feel we could trust with the position, and we have a desperate need," my response was immediate.

Since then we have sensed the hand of God on our lives not only for ministry in America and Canada, but also globally. Everything we're doing today really comes out of a heart relationship with God over a long period of time that has consistently moved us in this direction.

———

Chonda Pierce is best known as a comedian; her video, Having a Girls' Nite Out, *is one of the best-selling Christian comedy videos of all time. She has also authored several books that are as insightful as they are humorous. I asked Chonda if it's important for her to define her mission in life.*

Chonda Pierce

I don't think of myself as having a "grand mission." That would be thinking a little too highly of myself. Who am I? Now Paul—*he* had a mission. I look at people like Paul and say, "There's somebody that the Lord really planted here." I don't know if it's my own dysfunction or my insecurity, but I have a tough time saying that about myself.

I know I am here on this earth to love God. Sometimes I do it privately, and sometimes I get to do it in front of people. My relationship with Him is an open book. Out of that book I like to express the joy and fun of who God is. I guess I'm here to make people laugh because they need it!

I don't put any limits on where God can use me. Every moment is a moment that I breathe because of God. I used to teach Sunday school and was perfectly happy doing it. I was perfectly resigned to raising my kids at home, being an at-home mom. I had this plan: I'll be an at-home mom until the kids start school, then I'll get a part-time job so I can work while they're in school and be home when they're at home. It just didn't happen according to the plan.

I wrote a mission statement and hung it on the wall in my office. My brother told me that's something a person should do. It's good to give some thought to why you're doing what you're doing. But defining what I do, that's tough. People put me in categories: I'm a speaker, I'm a comedian, I'm an author, I'm a mother. I've never been able to put myself in a category. The entertainment industry will do it real quick for you because they have to. They don't know how to market somebody who does "whatever." That's not a marketable category. There's no Dove Award for that.

———

Author Karyn Henley has been creating wonderful children's books for two decades. Her international bestseller, The Beginners Bible, *has sold millions of copies and been translated into seventeen languages. Karyn explains that seeing the fruits of her labor is the heart of purpose for her.*

Karyn Henley

Writing books for children is the thing that most motivates me—communicating my heart to a child. When you want to write or communicate to a young person, you have to look back at your own childhood and remember that there is still a child in you. If I can make myself smile or giggle or shiver or say "wow"—if I can touch the child in me—then I know I'm making a good start toward touching another child with that same emotion.

When you really want to communicate a "wow" to children, you have to give them something that they can see in their mind and imagination. You have to give them something they can smell, something they can taste, something they can hear. That's the point in telling a good story, whether you're telling it verbally or trying to communicate it through the printed word. Either way, what you're going for is to have the children look at you or the words on the page and actually not see you or those words. They don't see the author; they don't see the teller; they just see the story. It is so vivid that they actually see it playing out in their minds as the words go by.

That's what I strive for, and reaching that goal is the most satisfying and meaningful thing for me. Having children actually see what I'm seeing, smell what I'm smelling, hear what I'm hearing, taste what I'm tasting—that's the motivation for me.

A grandmother wrote me a letter that included a photograph of her grandchild asleep on the bed with *The Beginners Bible* in his arms. I don't know—maybe the book was so boring that it put him to sleep! Actually the grandmother told me how much he enjoyed it. I consider it a special treasure when parents tell me their children pick up the book and don't want to put it down. They want to read it all the way through, and when they finish they want to read it again and again and again. As a writer who has studied writing and knows about books, I know that if a child wants to pick up a book again, that means the writer has done his or her job.

A lot of people look at the numbers and say, "You sold this many or that many books." To me, the best part is not the numbers. The best part is when I see children who are excited about what they are reading, and I realize that the Lord used me to express something to their hearts. That's where the rubber meets the road. For me, that's the treasure.

———————

Tony Campolo is a professor of sociology at Eastern College in St. Davids, Pennsylvania. He is also an ordained minister and a prolific author. Here Tony explains what it means to be "called."

Tony Campolo

The concept of calling is a strange one to me. It seems to me that the minute you become a Christian, you are called. Jesus didn't say, "Go ye into all the world and preach the gospel—if you are called." He said, "Go ye into all the world and preach the gospel." Period. He didn't say to love one another if you're called, to reach out to the poor if you're called; He didn't put those qualifications on His commandments.

Thus I contend that every Christian is called. Every Christian is called to be a missionary. Every Christian is called to express God's love and His sacrifice to others. As to how you work that out on an individual basis, it seems to me quite clear, is that you take advantage of every opportunity that comes your way, and you try to optimize those opportunities.

I find that young people often experience "paralysis in analysis." I watch them in Christian colleges wringing their hands and saying, "God has not revealed to me what His will is for my life." I don't know that the Bible ever said that God will reveal His will for our lives. Where in the Scriptures does it say that? Quite the opposite. The Bible says, "Sufficient unto the day is the evil thereof."

Let's ask, What does God want me to do today, *now*, with the options that are available to me and the opportunities that present themselves? If we are faithful in the little things day by day, the Scripture says, then He will make us rulers over great things. Then other things will fall into their place.

What's the Secret?

Building our lives around God's plan for us makes life an exciting and mysterious adventure in which the faith to move forward soon becomes treasure itself! And along with that treasure comes a meaningful relationship with God, a sure purpose, and the kind of happiness you and I will never find alone.

Secret #2

We Have to Start Out like We Want to End Up

Sometimes my mind wanders. Who knows what brings on such thinking? But sometimes I imagine myself lying in a hospital bed as an old, old man many years in the future. I'm dressed in one of those ugly, blue, hospital-issue gowns—you know, the ones that cover three-fourths of your body, leaving the rest of you exposed (and I don't mean your knees). Even now I can almost feel the scratchy acrylic texture of the hospital pillow beneath my head and the agitating presence of the oxygen tube under my nose. The room is quiet. I lie still, listening to the steady sound of the heart monitor ticking off the last "blips" of my life.

It may sound maudlin, but I wonder what I'll be thinking that day. What questions will I ask myself? "Did I live my life as I was meant to live it?" "Did I mess up my chance to do something important?" In the recesses of my mind I keep this picture tacked up—me as an old man in a hospital bed. It reminds me of the obvious: The day will come when I can't do anything to change the answers to those questions. But today I still can.

We each have a past, a present, and a future, and in their roomy margins we write the story of our life. That's the movie we believe we'll see in heaven one day, and it's in production today. We are both the star and the screenwriter. We come up with the words we speak to loved ones and strangers alike. We determine the tone, the plot, and the rating. Whether our movie is gracious and civilized or coarse and vulgar, we're on the set each day making it happen.

Sometimes life is a comedy. Sometimes it's a tragedy, a love story, and a drama all wrapped up into one big show. Whatever it is, we have the opportunity to play one of the "good guys"—one who lives by a clear moral code, who infuses the film with purpose. Jesus, of course, is the ultimate "good guy." He can do no wrong. He's our example. He's the one we should strive to be like as our movie is filmed day by day.

None of us can change our past; that's why regret is such a prevalent emotion in our world. But we can change our present and our future. These aren't fixed yet. They're still moldable, adaptable—our days of grace. We still have time to shape them into the legacy we desire. As a pastor's wife I know likes to say, we just have to "start out like we want to end up."

If our intent is to end up with God, we need to start out in the direction of the Good Road. And while its name certainly portends a good destination, the views seen along this road are good as well. Love, joy, peace, patience, kindness, and the other "sights" provided by the Holy Spirit (Galatians 5:22–23) can only be experienced on the Good Road. If we start out as lovers of God and of each other, we'll see those sights, stand in awe of their wonders, draw strength from their resting places, and ultimately follow that Good Road home.

In this chapter I asked the authors, "How did you start out?" I wanted to know about their unique upbringings, their formative years, their family life. Did they begin on the Good Road, or did they have to find their way later in life? I asked, "What in your 'starting out' was most instrumental in making you the person you are today?"

Seeing how history has molded those people we hold in high esteem is always illuminating. Not only is our image of them clearer, but their recollections jog memories of our own. We find ourselves considering what shaped *us*—what events along the way formed us into the men and women we've become. We realize that simple, everyday incidents can have long-lasting impact when they touch the soul. Seemingly insignificant moments between a parent and a child, for example, may be remembered for a lifetime, marking the instant when a ministry is born.

Life experiences can take us in different directions, but the choices we make today determine, in large part, our destinations tomorrow. Do we want to take the Good Road, see awesome sights along the way, and end up at home with a heavenly Father who loves us? Do we want His best for our lives? Then beginning today, let's start out like we want to end up.

Probably the number one question writers are asked is, "How did you get started?" Here Karyn Henley shares her story and points to her childhood as the place where she got her start.

Karyn Henley

I think there was always some writing in my blood. My mother used to write for Sunday schools, and as I grew up she read to my three little sisters and me all the time. I think a writer is first of all a reader, and when you grow up reading and you grow up with words, books are special to you. It's in your blood.

Still, I didn't think of being a writer until I became a teacher. I knew I enjoyed kids and wanted to work with them, so I went to college and got a degree in education with a certificate in Early Childhood. (At that point I was really most interested in working with the little guys.) I got married right out of college, and my husband and I moved to California. I got my first teaching job at a private preschool; it wasn't a Christian school, but it gave me a lot of experience with the young kids.

I would read to the class every day—I guess because my mom had read to me, and I knew how special that was. And at some point I started thinking, *You know, I would really enjoy writing something for children.* I started looking into the possibility. I began reading about writing, taking a course in writing for children, and trying my hand at submitting little articles here and there. I got a couple of articles published at different places, and I got my first book published by the Carolrhoda Company in Minneapolis. That's not a Christian company. I didn't start out to write Christian material; I was just writing for kids. My first book was published the same year my first child was born, so that was a big year for me—two babies, and they both took a lot of labor!

Patsy Clairmont is a humorist, a best-selling author, and a speaker at the hugely successful Women of Faith conferences, addressing tens of thousands of women each year. Here Patsy talks about how she started out. You may be surprised.

Patsy Clairmont

It blesses my heart to think that I would have something of value to offer another life. You see, I was a high school dropout and a teenage runaway. I was married by the time I turned seventeen, and I had my first child at twenty. I became housebound with agoraphobia [the fear of open spaces]. Those are not exactly the kind of credentials you would expect for someone who is addressing so many people, who has the privilege of writing and speaking to such large audiences.

But I have been a seeker of truth—first because of the extent of my own brokenness, and second because of my limited educational background. Long ago, when I was in such deep distress at so many levels of my life, I began reading everything I could get my hands on, and God began using that. It was as if I was in a gazillion different puzzle pieces. Then He would send a book or a tape along—something that only He could have known I needed at that moment—through the hands of someone who may not have known anything at all about my predicament. And slowly He began to fit the pieces together. Of course the thing that has been most beneficial has been the Word of God. I tell people it's the glue that holds this old cracked pot together. He used the counsel of His Word to help establish me and give me some balance emotionally.

How does someone with a background like Patsy's become a nationally known speaker and author? I asked her to talk about that process in her life.

People often come up and say to me, "I want to do what you do." And I think, *oh boy*. I tell them right off the bat, "You know what? I didn't know this was what I was going to do when I grew up." When I was a little girl, I had a dream in my heart of being a writer; but when I grew up to be a failure, the dream went away. There wasn't any reason for me to ever consider it again.

But in my brokenness and desperation, I began to seek answers for my life. And when I stopped thinking I had all the answers, He began answering all my questions! That was a tremendous step for me, moving from A to B—from having all the answers when I really knew nothing, to having all the questions because I was so obviously in need.

"God's little bookie"

As I opened myself up for God's answers, I became very excited about reading books. I even started a little bookstore in my home to feed my habit. I needed to continue to grow and learn, and I didn't have the finances to provide myself with all the books I wanted. I had read all my friends' libraries. With my own bookstore, I could read a book before I sold it!

I got so excited about all the different books and authors that I began going into churches at their invitation and telling them about different books. I became a book reviewer. Soon I was being called "God's little bookie." I started giving my reviews at retreats, and pretty soon people were asking me to emcee. Then they were asking me to do a workshop and then a main session.

At about that time, [Christian author and speaker] Florence Littauer came along in my life. Everywhere Florence would speak, people would ask her if she could recommend other speakers for future events. So she decided that she would hand-select thirty-five women from across the United States, train them as speakers, and teach them what it had taken her years to learn. Of course, she has extensive credentials and several degrees. She happened to come to a retreat where I was doing book reviews, and she said, "Little girl, come with me." She took me home with her, and she began investing her rich educational background into my life. So God gave me the rest of my high school education in book form, and then He gave me a college education in "Florence form." We even traveled together for ten years, training other people in communication skills.

getting the words on a page

One day I got a call from Focus on the Family. I'd spoken to a group of Quaker women, and one of the women had sent the tape to the ministry. Now Focus wanted to know if they could air the tape on their national radio program. Well, much to my amazement, the thing took off like gangbusters. It became one of the most requested tapes in the history of their broadcast. So then Focus asked if I would like to write a book. I told them, "Writing a book has been my dream since I was a little girl. But I have to be honest with you—I really don't know how to make my words go onto the written page."

"Don't worry," they said. "We think we can direct you onto the page."

So I agreed, but I told them, "This would be my longing and

request: that you would not do my rewrite work but teach me how to do my own."

Of course, I didn't know what I was asking for. I didn't know how unusual such a request was. Nor did I realize at that point—as I do now in hindsight—that the process would become the writing courses I had missed out on. Some of the "cracked pot" stories [from her first book, *God Uses Cracked Pots*] are tiny, little snippets, but I had to write some of them six different times before they were ready for print. In the process of having to write and rewrite and write and rewrite, I learned how to express myself on the written page.

———

Henry Blackaby's strong commitment to Christ is evident in both his books and his teaching. It's fascinating to peer into Henry's childhood and see how his parents and faithful family helped bring him up to be the man of God he is today.

Henry Blackaby

My dad was a layman; he worked in the Bank of Montreal. But he also started several churches as a layman because we had no one who wanted to be our pastor. He was very committed as a deacon most of his life, and he saw in the New Testament that deacons, like Philip and Steven, preached. He knew that preaching was a part of his responsibility. If there was no evangelical church in the area, he knew he was responsible for asking God to guide him to start one.

The origins of my own ministry were there—with my father preaching, my mother playing the piano, my older brother ushering, and my younger brother and I being the congregation! God laid a burden on my heart for the nation [Canada]. I had a faithful family behind me, and they did more than any other single thing to shape who I am as a person.

———

Small, seemingly insignificant experiences from childhood can have an enormous effect on us as we mature. Larry Crabb, whose most recent ministry focus has been on deepening relationships inside the church, recalls a particular childhood memory that still shapes him today.

Larry Crabb

I can remember when I was six years old. Dad was quite a tennis player, and he would take my older brother, Bill, and me to the tennis courts. We would watch Dad, his brother, and two other guys play doubles every Tuesday night. The wives would bring the coffee and refreshments, and we'd have a little picnic. It was a wonderful family time.

But I can remember watching Dad play tennis and noticing that sometimes he said things that were designed—from my perspective as a six-year-old—to help him feel like he was more a part of things. Cracking jokes that weren't terribly funny, maybe. I remember thinking, *Dad, I know you long to fit in. But don't apologize for yourself; don't try so hard to make it happen.* At six years old I saw that it is so important to belong; it's so important to feel like you're one of the team, one of the guys. I've struggled with this all my life. I've had this longing to connect, this longing to feel deeply close. And that's one of the ways God has shaped my calling.

———

Of the many wonderful speakers featured in this book, Tony Campolo is one of the best. Born, raised, and still living in Philadelphia, Tony is part of a proud Italian family that taught him the value of pursuing goodness rather than happiness or success.

Tony Campolo

I was born in Philadelphia, raised in Philadelphia, and went to school in Philadelphia. I've never worked anyplace but here. I'm Italian, and there is a tradition within our community to stay put, to stay with the extended clan. I'm very much a part of that. That's who I am.

When I ask Japanese parents what they want their children to be when they grow up, I get one standard answer: "successful." No society has driven its children to succeed as much as the Japanese have; they are successful at everything. When I ask American mothers the same question, I get one standard answer: "happy." I grew up in an ethnic Italian family, and if you would have asked my parents years ago what they wanted their son to be when he grew up, they would've said "good." They would not have used the word *happy*.

When a society is oriented toward happiness rather than goodness, it's in trouble. And unfortunately, in America we have a generation of young people who are committed to being happy. That's a terrible commitment! Their marriages can't work; the first time they are unhappy, they want out. I constantly hear, "I'm getting a divorce. We're just not happy." They can't stay in jobs; the minute they are unhappy at work, they quit.

The truth is our young people have a tendency to be so hungry for happiness that they are never content with where they are. They are never satisfied with what they have. They always think that there is greater happiness waiting for them somewhere down the pike. But I contend that if you seek first the kingdom of God and His righteousness, then all of the other things will take care of themselves—including happiness.

———

Obviously, the environment we grow up in has a big part in shaping our lives. Sheila Walsh grew up in a quaint fishing village in Scotland. Her upbringing there taught her how to be fruitful in God's kingdom and prepared her to sing and speak in front of huge audiences all over the world.

Sheila Walsh

I'm very grateful to have been born in Scotland, just as I am grateful now to live in America. I grew up without a lot of money but with a lot of love and a lot of friendship. One of the good things about having a childhood in Scotland is that life is very simple there. It's not nearly as complicated as we make it out to be over here nowadays.

Most people in Scotland remain in the same towns, so when I go back home my mother is still there; my sister is there; my aunts, my uncles, and my cousins are there. People have an extended community. You don't find as many people in Scotland going to therapists because they have a family to talk to. A lot of the people in America are lonely, so they end up going to a therapist or counselor or pastor because they don't have anyone else they can trust or talk to.

I'm also very grateful that I grew up in a country where there are very few Christians. Only 2 percent of the population in Scotland goes to church. I think that when you are a very small light in the midst of the darkness, you have to make sure your light is shining brightly. When you grow up in a country where there are Christian schools, Christian TV stations, Christian everything, you may not even notice when your light gets a little dim.

But when I went to high school, the only other Christian there was a French teacher. That was wonderful for me because it made me really struggle with my faith. It gave me a great passion to share my faith with others, and I started a very simple Bible study. By the end of my senior year, there were forty-five of us in that group. I am very grateful to have been brought up in a place where it wasn't easy to be a Christian but where some of the more basic values of life were very strong.

———————

I tend to expect that Christians involved in ministry are the products of solid Christian homes. That's clearly not always the case. Steve Brown takes us back to the home he grew up in to show us how God is present even in imperfect situations.

Steve Brown

I'm a second-generation bastard. That's not a cussword; that's a word with a definition that applies to my father. Nobody knew who my father's father was, and yet my father taught me unconditional love. He became a Christian just three months before he died; but he had always been kind, even though he was a drunk. He did a lot of bad things, but he always loved his boys, and he showed it in every way possible. His love was always unconditional.

My father started out without a father. In those days they called it being "illegitimate." Being illegitimate lays a trip on you, and it definitely had an impact on our family. Dad was an alcoholic, as a lot of people in his family were, and his brother was a bank embezzler. (I've got a wonderful background! You didn't expect this, did you?)

My mother came from a good family, but all three of her sisters married alcoholics. Mom was earthly and godly in the best sense of those words. Mean as a snake, but she loved God with all her heart! She tithed when we didn't have money to tithe. When she became a Christian she decided that tithe was going to belong to God, and her commitment had a tremendous influence on our lives.

It's an interesting thing. I am not a good person, and I would like to drink, to be honest with you. I've always thought it would be sophisticated to be able to go into a restaurant and order a bottle with a French-sounding name and let everybody know how much I know. But I've never been able to drink. All wines taste like Kool-Aid gone bad to me. I've really tried, and I'm not proud of it. But for some reason I was the generation that saw a lot of that bondage to alcohol broken because of God's grace. I'll be eternally grateful for that.

My wife and I have been married thirty-eight years. We have two daughters, both of whom are married. One works in our ministry here, and the other lives in Birmingham, Alabama. We have two granddaughters who are just wonderful. You know those old guys who are always showing pictures of their grandkids, and you want to tell them, "Here's a quarter—go call someone who cares"? Well, I understand now. I have this deal where I'll show you my pictures and I'll let you show me yours. My family has gone through a lot of bad stuff. We've fought, we've failed, and we've stayed together—and I wouldn't trade it for anything.

Max Lucado is the pulpit minister of the Oak Hills Church of Christ in San Antonio, Texas, and one of the preeminent Christian authors of our day. Here he tells the story of a man whose commitment to Christ followed a personal struggle with alcohol.

Max Lucado

Well, you know, I'm an old converted drunk. I was well on the road to alcoholism by the time I was eighteen. Giving up drinking the summer of my senior year in high school was a very profound moment for me. Though it was not the moment that I gave my life to Christ, it was the moment that I turned away from a road that was leading me into a lot of trouble. It would be two years before I gave my heart to Christ.

With the exception of my own father, for which I'm very grateful, my father's family struggled with alcoholism. We have it all over our family tree. I'm convinced beyond a doubt that had the Lord not intervened, I was headed down that same road. So that moment in my senior year when I had drunk a six-pack and couldn't feel it— I had gotten so resistant to alcohol that I couldn't feel it—I turned to my friend in the front of his pickup truck in Andrews, Texas, and said, "There's got to be more to life than this." That was a turning point for me.

My decision to follow Christ occurred when I was in college. I was a sophomore at Abilene Christian University in Abilene, Texas. One of the things that had held me back from making a commitment to Christ sooner was the old excuse that people who say they're Christians don't always act like it. I figured I could act better than most of them did. I figured that when and if I became a Christian, I was going to take it seriously.

When some friends invited me to spend the summer of my junior year in Brazil, I felt the Lord calling my hand. I was deeply touched by the work of the missionaries I met and decided I'd like to do the same. I never intended to go into a full-time ministry. I figured that I'd go down to Brazil for about five years and do mission work then come back and go into some form of business or maybe to law school.

As things turned out, I stayed on at school to do some preparatory work for being a missionary. But while pursuing my master's degree in Bible, I was exposed to pastoral work. By the time I moved to Brazil in 1983, I knew I would love to be a minister. I still had a high regard and admiration for those who spend their whole lives encouraging churches in foreign countries. But I went to Brazil knowing I'd be a missionary only a few years. My desire was to eventually go into full-time church work back in the United States.

I was in Rio de Janeiro, Brazil, for five years, from 1983 to 1988. The big challenge was trying to figure out what we in our church had to offer the Brazilians. Though Brazil is primarily Catholic, the real religion there is spiritism—a mystical, very emotional religion associated with voodoo and seances. Many of the high-power, high-profile people in Brazil are spiritists. The question we had to wrestle with was this: What do we have to offer them that spiritism does not? We came to the conclusion that we offered forgiveness of sins and victory over death, which is the heart of the gospel. That clarified for us what our message was. I've often felt that I got a lot more out of going to Brazil than the Brazilians ever got out of me going to Brazil. My theology and my message was distilled down to those two things: forgiveness and eternal life.

———

Here's an interesting story about events that come full circle. It takes place in the rainy city of Seattle. Its backdrop is the aviation industry of the 1950s, and it has two main characters: a father who leaves the ministry because of his son, and a son who enters the ministry because of his father.

Frank Peretti

My dad started out as a pastor. Both he and my mom went to Northwest Bible Institute in Seattle back in 1948. He pastored one church in Whitehall, Montana, and one up near Westbridge, Alberta, in Canada. When I was born in 1951, I was injured and needed hospitalization, so my folks moved to Seattle and got me into the children's orthopedic hospital there. While we were in

Seattle, Dad left the ministry and got a job working for the Boeing Company. He ended up working at Boeing for the next thirty years.

My injury was such that it produced a tumor on the side of my neck. They operated on the tumor, but then the problem spread to my tongue and it became life-threatening. I had to have all kinds of surgeries. I didn't really recover from all this stuff until about the seventh grade. It was a long process to get my tongue and my mouth all straightened out. My parents did a lot of praying. They even took me to Oral Roberts for prayer. I don't remember going, but I remember hearing them tell me about it.

Dad's job was building Boeing airplanes. If I may editorialize a little bit, we often tend to look at life through an idealistic, rose-colored, everything's-going-to-be-cool kind of a perspective. Dad got a job at Boeing because he had to make a living. It was that simple. Those are the simple nuts and bolts of life. He couldn't pastor anymore because I was in the hospital, and there were expenses to be met. Now as to why he stayed at Boeing—it would be interesting to ask him. I would guess it was because he had a family and responsibilities, and it seemed the best thing to do.

What's interesting is the end of the story. When he was about fifty-five, Dad retired from the Boeing Company and went back into the ministry. And when he did, he and I pastored a church together! So it was a bookend-ish kind of a thing, a return to the Promised Land after being in Egypt—however you want to look at it. He left the ministry because of me and worked for thirty years at Boeing. Then when he returned to the ministry, I returned with him.

Grant Jeffrey is the founder of Frontier Research and the best-selling author of numerous books dealing with prophecy and the Bible. I asked him to talk about his background and explain what started his intense interest in prophetic matters.

Grant Jeffrey

Back when I was a teenager growing up in Ottawa, Canada, my dad took me to prophecy conferences. He loved to talk about prophecy and current events, and it was very natural for me to view prophecy as fascinating because it dealt with the future. I remember witnessing to friends and using prophecy as a proof that the Bible was inspired. It struck me as very obvious that prophecy, humanly speaking, was impossible. What are the odds of guessing the exact score of a football game being played tomorrow? No psychic would be foolish enough to risk his or her reputation trying! Yet the Bible contains thousands of accurate prophecies in great detail.

I began collecting books about prophecy in my teens. When I went to Philadelphia College of Bible at sixteen, I found some wonderful little bookstores. I started buying old books because they were cheaper, but I soon found that many of the great writers of past centuries had more to say to me than many of the newer authors in Christian bookstores. Perhaps that's because the old writers had no television, no radio, and few distractions. What could you do when the night settled in and all you had was a candle or lantern? Well, you read or talked or thought until you finally slept. Many of these writers were not even pastors but laymen with a profound love for the Word; yet they were given insights by God that seemed much more profound to me than any of the more modern ideas I was reading in the college bookstore.

Fortunately, as I said, the old books were ridiculously inexpensive. Many of the books I bought back in those early collecting years cost five dollars or less, even though they were often leather-bound volumes hundreds of years old. Now, of course, that's no longer the case. I have to travel the world to find really excellent old books that deal with prophecy.

But over the years, as I read and studied those old writers, God placed a profound love of the Word of God in my heart and a desire to share that love with others. And I found out very quickly that if I wanted to share Christ and I talked about prophecy, most people would listen. Prophecy has value, not only because it points to Jesus Christ and the plan of redemption but because it makes sense. It answers the larger questions about why God is doing what He is doing in history. It also proves to non-Christians in a very simple way that the Bible is supernatural. I find that unbelievers can see that argument much more clearly than they can, say, an explanation of creation over evolution.

Tragically, fewer than one Christian in one hundred has the patience or interest to actually read enough creation research to become convinced intellectually that evolution is a fraud, even though material is ample and excellent. But in the minds of most people, prophecy piques a natural interest. Even those who have no religious feelings whatsoever will listen to you talk about prophecy. It is an incredibly good apologetic tool.

The memories we carry out of childhood are so important. They stay with us forever and help make us who we are. Listening to some of Barbara Johnson's memories begs the question: What memories are we planting in the hearts of our own children?

Barbara Johnson

My dad was a minister. The church used to have campaigns, and he'd travel around like Billy Graham does, ministering in tents with hard benches and sawdust-covered floors. My dad was the song leader, so I would sing too. I was so young and so small; he would stand me on a chair and then hold me so I wouldn't fall off. Kids would sit there swinging their feet, kicking the sawdust, and making their folks so mad! But that was the only thing you could do with the sawdust—kick it.

Whenever I go anywhere now and smell lumber shavings, I'm reminded of that old sawdust trail. Memories that you put in the heart of a child can never be erased. They are always there.

What's the Secret?

Whatever our pasts, there's a bright future beckoning us. All we have to do is start out—from this point forward—like we want to end up. And the only place worth ending up is in the arms of a loving heavenly Father. Let's make sure we get there!

God Has Placed Family and Friends in Our Lives to Love

This current season of life, though hectic and often overburdened with obligations, is the best one yet for me. Since giving my life to Christ many years ago and continually deepening that commitment as time goes by, each year just seems to get better.

Having said that, if I could go back in time to any year of my life and enjoy a moment all over again, I would want to go back to 1987 and a backyard barbecue that took place during my summer break from college. The memory comes back to me audibly first: the sizzle of hamburgers and hot dogs grilling on the hibachi, music playing on the stereo, the rich laughter of dear friends. Then the picture comes into focus: The day is sunny; the apartment patio is open and breezy. My friends look much younger, more carefree, full of good health and potential, as we recline together in the shade of our own slice of heaven—a warm summer day that is ours to keep! We talk about nothing, and the nothing is perfect; our souls soak up the pleasure of just spending time with each other.

It's the kind of day that is unusually long and still somehow too short, a day now perfected in my memory. I doubt I've tampered with it much over the years. It was perfect the first time it came around, and it still is perfect every time I remember it.

Every great recollection makes its way into the Memory Hall of Fame on the shoulders of the people in it. Personally, I can't imagine living without my family and friends. Nothing makes sense outside of my relationships with them. Except for my relationship with Christ, there is nothing I prefer or value over people. No possession takes precedence—nor could it—over my loved ones.

The late founder of Wal-mart, Sam Walton, once remarked, "If you're going to be in business long, you'd better like people, because that's all we've got around here." That's true not only in business but in all of life. Every day we spend time interacting with others. Our best memories are best because they're experienced with people. Birthdays, weddings, anniversaries, Father's Day, Mother's Day, Valentine's Day—these are all holidays that center on people and our relationships with them.

In heaven, which is life perfected, we will still have relationships. We will recognize and know one another. In fact, our relationships are the only things that will go with us into eternity, thus proving their importance to God and showing us how valuable they should be to us on earth.

Yes, people are all we've got around here, and they all matter to God. We can lavish love upon people because of their importance to Jesus. We can invest ourselves in their lives because loving God and loving others are God's first and second commandments to us. And we can try to shake off the self-loathing that some of us have picked up along the way and give ourselves a break too.

After all, God gives us good things to enjoy in life—food, fishing, football, the arts, music, travel, books, conversation, the company of good friends, and countless other activities. Yet some of us refuse to stop working long enough to smell the roses God has planted in our life's garden. We work ourselves into sleeplessness and then wonder why life seems so unbearable and hectic. My prayer for each of us, as the authors share these snapshots from their lives, is that we will grow to appreciate rest, relaxation, and the people around us—and especially those closest to us. The ones we love most are sometimes the ones we forget first when we busy ourselves with the distractions of life. But it is in our relationships with family and friends that we find the secret to true happiness and fulfillment.

While we may have an intellectual understanding of God's love, we can never grasp its full magnitude with our minds. That's where relationships come in. Spending time with the people we love helps us to more fully understand—with our hearts—the love God has for us.

Sheila Walsh

I see my son, Christian, almost as a parable. It's as if I'm seeing the unfolding mercy and goodness of God when I look at my child—as if I'm holding thirty-one-and-a-half pounds of the grace of God in my arms every day. People said to me before Christian was born that he would give me a fresh understanding of the love of God, and I made a mental assent to that at the time. But I didn't even begin to understand the depth of how that is true. I would literally lie down in front of a car and die for Christian. I would do anything in this world to love and protect him. And I think that is just a tiny, flawed, human shadow of the passion that God feels toward us.

Christian has helped me understand grace. One of the things I say to Christian every night is, "I love your ears, I love your eyes, I love your nose, I love your toes. I love you when you're good, I love you when you're naughty, I love you when you're happy, I love you when you're sad." I don't always approve of everything he does—like when he takes my pale blue suede pumps and flushes them down the toilet —but it doesn't stop me from loving him. I understand the same about God now. There are times when I'll make God happy, and there are times when I'll make God sad, but He never stops loving me.

———————◆———————

Our relationship with God, our relationships with other people, and even the way we relate to ourselves can be restored by the miraculous work of the gospel. Larry Crabb explains why our relationships are a fundamental aspect of who we are in Christ.

Larry Crabb

Once you take seriously what one theologian has called the cornerstone of the Christian religion—the Trinity, that God Himself exists as a relationship—you realize that God is fundamentally a relational God. John Piper wrote a wonderful book, *The Pleasures of God: Meditations on God's Delight in Being God,* in which he talks about God's delight in being God. He's having a good time with Each Other! I don't know how to put that into proper language; it's one God and three Persons. It's the mystery of the Trinity. But He really enjoys the community of the three Persons of the Godhead. I believe He created people so they could enjoy the same kind of relationship, because that's what is eternal, that's what is bedrock, that's what is ontologically final.

The conservative wing of the church has put the pulpit in the center as a way of saying that what matters is not community but its proclamation. My judgment is that proclamation is crucial in order to move us toward community—but *community* is the central thing. The liberal wing of the church has not moved relationship into the center either. Rather, it has made things like achievement, position, and prestige central, and that has caused a reaction. Now the postmodern reformation has moved toward a kind of phony spirituality in which we're talking more about community but without the gospel as its basis.

The thing that's eternal, that's going to last, is connection, relationship. To me the words are synonymous. Relationship is fundamental because God is the source of all relationships.

When I relate to Him, then I can really relate to myself honestly. I can admit when I'm a pain in the neck, I can admit when I'm a phony, and I can admit when I'm a failure. I can face what's true about me because nothing that's true about me destroys me; the gospel has made me indestructible. Therefore I can face myself without pretense, and then I can relate to you. When you drive me nuts, I can still celebrate you, because Christ is in you.

That brings the whole thing back to the way it was designed to be: full connection with God, with ourselves, and with each other. That's going to be heaven!

———————

Communication is essential for good relationships. It's the conduit through which we exchange ideas, pass on love and caring, and express our deepest selves. Karyn Henley has spent a lifetime learning and teaching the art of family communication. She gives us a glimpse of how communication works in the relationships closest to her.

Karyn Henley

The most satisfying thing for me is having unity and relationship as a family—being able to communicate with each other as family members. Communication is so important to me. It's important to have open lines of communication between me and my husband, between us as parents and our children, and even between our children among themselves. We have two sons. Last night I was listening to them communicate just between the two of them, and it was a treasure to me to hear real communication going on. Sometimes we have disagreements, but then the resolution follows and we move forward. We work together as a family.

We homeschooled our sons since the time our oldest was in kindergarten, and they've grown up helping us in the business, which is the business of communicating. They have traveled with us as we've done our seminars with teachers and parents. Our older son is working now in video communication. His vision is to go into film. Our younger son communicates in the field of acting. Both of them also have a home-grown degree in child education, because they have heard me speak over and over again. They really know about young children, about the growing child. They will sometimes step in and say, "Well, you know the preschooler really needs this or that in order to understand." That is very satisfying for me. They both are very good with children, and I envision the Lord will use that skill as they grow and develop in their careers.

———

A big part of loving our children is helping them come to faith in the One we've placed our faith in. Chonda Pierce talks about the differences in her children and how she and her husband, David, have tried to make God accessible to them.

Chonda Pierce

Every parent wants to believe they have an exceptional child. I do think I have one in Chera Kay. She's not a typical teenager. I don't have any problems. She has never come home with purple hair or four earrings. I'm really blessed. Now Zachary is on his way, so I better knock on wood before I go bragging on Chera. The teenage life—it cracks me up! There's material from my kids' lives I would love to use because it's so funny. Their lives are such a big deal! But I could never use stuff about Chera. I know her disposition; it would totally embarrass and devastate her, and I cannot do that. There are some people who will get a laugh at any cost. I won't pay that price.

Now Zachary is a different personality. He's always coming to me and saying, "Mom, I did this at school today. Be sure and use it tomorrow, OK? Because it was really stupid!" He's like, "Tell about me, tell about me!" And I thank the Lord that He gave me one of those. Oh yes, I can use anything that Zachary does. He loves it.

But Chera is incredible. She really loves the Lord, and I cry saying that. For years she has said that she wants to be a missionary. I took her to Guatemala last week, and even that experience didn't change her mind! I thought for sure she'd see a real mission field and say, "Oh yuck. I'm not going to be a missionary!" But she's ready to go now—tomorrow.

With no help from Mom, no prodding, no putting a star on the good girl chart, she adores the Lord. She's found a personal relationship with Him. She reads her Bible, and her knowledge of the Lord is a blessing. She has won several kids to the Lord. She never misses a day carrying her Bible to school. She has been ridiculed, poked fun at about it, and once in a while comes home teary-eyed. But she is so determined to save the world for Jesus. I don't know how I got so lucky! I talked to her about it on the flight to Guatemala: "Chera, what did I do right? What made you this way?"

here among us

God has always been a big topic in our home. He's been someone we talk to and about in front of our kids all the time. Our faith is not some mystical thing. My husband, David, and I have never closed our door and had devotions without our kids. They've seen us weep and cry, they've seen us fuss and fight, and they've seen us take it all before the Lord.

God is such a real deal in this house! From the time the kids were little, it has always been very natural for Jesus to crop up in conversation. I don't know how significant that has been in their lives, but I do know that David and I have tried to make a relationship with God very accessible to our children. We've wanted them to see firsthand that He is here among us. We've always read the Bible. My daughter has never listened to any music but Christian music in her life. If I'm in the car listening to 92.9 Easy Listening and she gets in, she says, "Mother, can you change the station, please?"

the meaning behind the madness

Chera has always been aware of why I do what I do. She knows my goal has never been to be a star. When I come home from a concert, we don't say, "We sold two thousand dollars worth of tapes. Praise the Lord!" We talk about what the Lord did that night. Were people encouraged? Did some people come to know Christ? We talk about the stories we hear at the book table after a concert. For example, one lady was facing a tough surgery the next week. She told me she had really needed the reprieve of laughter that she got that night. Isn't that great?

When we pack an envelope for somebody who ordered a *Girls' Nite Out* video, we say, "Isn't it amazing that this person would want this? Maybe they'll show it to an unbeliever." That's the meaning behind the madness of what I do—not "If we sold fifty thousand more of these we could get a gold-plated thing on the wall." David and I try to keep first things first, especially in front of our kids.

Do you know a good marriage when you see one? We are so hungry for role models who can demonstrate what a loving, lifetime commitment is supposed to look like! Here are two models:

Frank and Barbara Peretti. Their marriage exemplifies what real married love is like when it is lived in Christ.

Frank Peretti

I've been married to Barbara for twenty-seven years. We were married in 1972, when she was just eighteen and I was twenty-one. I had asked her to marry me when she was sixteen and I was nineteen, but we waited until she got out of high school! It's a good thing that we waited that long. Man, we were young! We are one of those teenage marriages that worked out. Well, I wasn't a teenager, but kids that age look really young to us now.

We grew together. We had the right mix of devotion and commitment. Love was more than just a warm, fuzzy feeling to us. It was a principle. It was a covenant, and we understood that even when we were that young.

We did go though years of struggle—not relationally, but occupationally. We went through years of trying to figure out what I was supposed to do with my life. I was a musician for a while, a carpenter, a printer. I did a lot of different things, and Barb just stuck with me until I finally connected as a writer. The dedication in *This Present Darkness* says, "To Barbara Jean, wife and friend. Who loved me and waited." Through the whole process, Barb waited. She loved me, and she never gave up on me. She stuck by me and waited until I finally got my act together and became the writer that God had wanted me to be in the first place.

That's one of the things that held us together and helped us to make it through life: the knowledge that God did have a plan and that we were sincerely seeking His will. I'm not going to say I made wrong turns. I think the Lord knew exactly what I was going to do and let me do it—that is, He let me be a musician for a while traveling around with bands; He let me work at carpentry; He let me be a printer. I went to UCLA for a while and studied film. I think the Lord was perfectly content to let me do all these things, because it gave me such a wonderful backlog of the experience of life itself. The lessons I learned were invaluable. I draw on all that stuff now as a writer.

I think it worked out great. I'm only forty-eight now. I've still got a lot more living to do, God willing. Barb and I can see that God had a plan for us from the beginning.

Brennan Manning was a Franciscan priest who eventually left his order and married. He speaks of his wife with an almost palpable love.

Brennan Manning

My wife, Roslyn, has been an extraordinary gift, an absolutely extraordinary gift. God sent me somebody to share His love, to cry me His tears, and to hold me tight in the Lord. He speaks to me more directly through her than through any other human being.

Family time is very important to prolific author Max Lucado. He talks about his love of family, his love of sports, and what happened during a period when he allowed his schedule to rule his life.

Max Lucado

I'm an exercise fanatic. I run about four miles every day, and I lift weights three or four times a week. I enjoy feeling and being healthy. One of the things I noticed when I got into preaching was how many fat preachers there are, and I decided I didn't want to be one. I try to keep my waistline down and look at least relatively healthy.

I love every sport. There's not one sport that I don't like. I go to a lot of Spurs basketball games and Cowboys football games. I really love golf.

I also have three terrific daughters, and it's a delight when I have an evening at home with them. I really protect my evenings. I'm out on Wednesday nights, and that's it. I know of other ministers who are out every night of the week. I leave my weeknights open for my girls' activities—basketball games, volleyball games, plays, stuff like that.

I don't travel. There was a time when I traveled so much that the American Airlines agents knew my first name; they really did. But I was in and out of the airport so often that I got burned out. I got insomnia. That was in 1994. At that point I started weaning myself off of the travel schedule, fulfilling obligations I had made but not accepting new ones. Last year I only took two or three speaking engagements. Something really has to be major for me to go now! This year I've accepted one engagement for my mother and one for a conference that our whole church staff is going to. The truth is, I just like to stay at home.

———

We live such busy lives that we must carve out time to rest and recharge. Our work is important, but so are we!

Tony Campolo

The greatest problem I have right now is that I don't unwind. I don't have off-hours and I don't take a Sabbath, which is a breaking of the commandment. I need to deal with that. My friends are really on me these days saying, "Hey, you can't go on like this, nonstop, forever. This is Satan's way of destroying you."

That is where I have to focus in and change. If I did have more time, the thing I would do is just go off with my wife, take long walks in beautiful places, and talk. That to me is unwinding.

———

I asked Grant Jeffrey what interests he has outside of Bible prophecy. Isn't it remarkable that when we're in God's will, we can find ourselves doing as work the very things we love?

Grant Jeffrey

It's funny. When you write about Bible prophecy, people assume that that's your only interest. I have many interests. I'm fascinated by politics, the military, history, technology, theology, archaeology—and in fact, I do write about all these things. I have more varied interests than anyone I know! I'm fascinated by the out-of-doors. I love boating, fishing, hunting, exploring. I love traveling the world with my wife, Kay, and interviewing world leaders and people involved in intelligence in the military. I have a zillion interests, and it's been a great blessing of God that the things that I've been interested in I've been able to write about and share with others, and they've found them interesting too.

———

God has made each of us unique, with our own favorite hobbies and interests. One of Scotty Smith's hobbies is fishing. I can just see Scotty and his son reeling in river trout as if they were in a scene from the movie A River Runs through It.

Scotty Smith

I have two children; my son is a freshman in college, and my daughter just got married this past year. My son and I love to fish together—all kinds of fishing: fly-fishing, spin fishing, ocean fishing, creek fishing, river fishing. I've especially enjoyed developing an understanding of fly-fishing with my son in recent years.

I also enjoy cooking shows. If I were on a desert island and I was told I could watch one hour of cable TV a day for the rest of my life, I would choose two cooking shows. I am fascinated with the culinary process. I am not a great chef, but I love to make fruit cobblers and breads and stuff like that. I enjoy food preparation, watching people make great food. I love to smell it, love to watch it, love to eat it.

I enjoy the creative process. I love going to watch an artist in our church create. I love listening to music. I grew up on the Beatles, the Beach Boys, classic rock-'n'-roll. I'm fascinated by creation. That's why I've enjoyed pondering God as Creator more than ever in recent years. I've gotten more excited than ever about the new creation, the new heavens and the new earth. I guess that's also why I love watching food being made and why I enjoy fly-fishing, which is far more a technical science than just putting a worm on a hook. In the last year I've taken up woodworking, and now I'm creating furniture with a few friends—learning how to turn trees into chests and tables and chairs. That's a new, fun thing for me.

I asked Scotty to address the subject of people in ministry taking time off. Because of the demands placed on pastors, ministers, missionaries, and laypeople, the temptation is to work nonstop. But those heavy demands are the very reason why it's critical to take time to recharge.

I used to have a real stultified understanding of the Christian life. Somewhere early on, part of me got the message that the noblest calling is to burn out for Jesus. Many years into the faith I realized there's no chapter and verse on burnout. In fact, one of my favorite stories in Scripture is of Jesus in the home of Mary and Martha. I can relate so much to Martha, who was busy doing things for Jesus, as opposed to Mary, who chose to spend her time communing with Him. Whether you are a pastor, a nuclear physicist, an earthworm rancher, a third-grade teacher—whatever your job— every single Christian is called to experience the fullness of life as God has made it known as Creator and Redeemer.

Martin Luther has become one of my favorite heroes in the faith. Luther—coming out of a very wrong view of the faith and wrong view of the clergy—went on to realize that if we really take the Scripture seriously, we will see that planting a tree and preaching the gospel are of equal worth in the sight of God. All of life is to be lived *coram deo*, before His face. Therefore, we're wrong to discriminate and say, "I'm called to 'holy duties.'" We're called to know Him and to walk with Him.

If God tells us—and He does in His Word—that His whole creation speaks of His glory, then we're called to enjoy it. Pastors are morons if they don't enjoy the very world they are instructing believers to be good stewards of. I don't have a lot of sympathy for pastors who get totally burned out on the ministry if they have not chosen to live life the way God has called them to live it; that is, to enjoy His pleasure and passion in every sphere of life. They are to give themselves—body, heart, soul, mind, and strength—to the preaching of the gospel. But more than that, they are to give themselves to the knowing of God in every texture, sphere, and aspect of life as He has made it.

———◆———

Whether we're involved in full-time ministry or not, we risk burning out when we scatter ourselves in too many directions. Henry Blackaby shares his secret for living an unhurried life.

Henry Blackaby

I never separate my work life from my personal life. Scripture says, "*He* is your life," and I try not to segment it. I think the people who segment—"Now I've got to do this; now I better give time to that"—are the ones who seem to burn out. I take it one day at a time. Though my schedule is very full and demanding, I try to live an unhurried and unpressured life. I don't let circumstances control me; I try to control the circumstances. When other people try to put deadlines on me, I do my best to meet some of them. But I don't let others set the course for the deadlines on my life. I try to walk with the Lord in an unhurried way.

It's a delight for me to be in different places, to be with different people, to have different assignments; and I integrate it all into one life. I think many leaders see their professional life, their personal life, and their family life as separate entities. They try to segment them. I don't do that at all. I simply enjoy everything as I go along.

What's the Secret?

We all need to spend time enjoying the life God has given us. Most of all, we need to love our family and friends. They're the ones who make our lives a satisfying and joyful journey.

Secret #4

A Calling from God Is a Labor of Love

I got my first job when I was seven years old. My older brother, Paul, was ten, and together we spent a day pitching boxes of all-occasion greeting cards door to door. He was the sales guy, and I pulled the wagon. As I recall, at the end of that long, hot, August day, Paul had made about six dollars, and he paid me in bubble gum. Later, when I was a little older, I inherited Paul's paper route, riding my bike a couple of hours each day after school, tossing newspapers. I delivered fifty papers a day and earned about forty-five dollars a week. I loved it.

My worst job? I waited tables at a country club after graduating from college when I couldn't find work in my field. It was honest labor, but I felt as if my work had no greater purpose—that I was working only for money. I wondered if I'd ever get to the vocation God had for me.

In earlier chapters we talked about the importance of building our lives around God's plans for us, starting out like we wanted to finish, and loving the family and friends God has placed in our lives.

An equally significant factor in a faith well lived is our attitude toward our work—that *something* toward which we direct our occupational energies. Whether we assemble automobiles in Detroit, pick oranges in Orlando, trade stocks on Wall Street, or sell goods on Main Street, our labor has the potential not only to benefit our society but to serve an even greater purpose.

Of course, it's obvious to us that someone like Billy Graham is called to his work. When we look at our own jobs, however, we often wonder how employment with the county school district, the city hospital, or the local post office can account for anything significant in the kingdom of God. But it can, because God's understanding of our individual and collective design infinitely exceeds our own. He is God, and we are not. He knows how everything can work together. It doesn't matter if He uses us to evangelize or to pray or to type or to sell or to sing; what does matter is that we do what we do in "faith expressing itself through love" (Galatians 5:6).

Let's say a man leaves his successful job on Wall Street and travels all the way to Africa to be a missionary—only to find that he isn't particularly good at it. So, after failing on the mission field, he returns to Wall Street, where he is spectacularly gifted at making money. He then channels the money he makes to those who are gifted missionaries in Africa but who lack resources. Now, being a missionary is thought of as highly religious work; being a Wall Street stockbroker, not religious. Nevertheless, if both are done in faith and expressed through love, using gifts given by God, aren't both worthy callings?

Since we spend so much of our lives working, it is important that we find meaningful work that we're well suited for. This can't be stressed enough. However, if we're already set in a job or career and confused about how it could be used for God's holy purposes, we need only to inquire of Him. The Bible says He offers wisdom if we ask (James 1:5). The adventure of following Christ is experienced more fully when the Holy Spirit is integrated into the work we perform. When Christ becomes our purpose and serving humanity our business, all of our skills, gifts, and positions are available tools for God to use to minister to each person we encounter.

This chapter focuses on the work to which the authors have dedicated themselves. I found that asking simple questions about their professions was a catalyst for new insights on the subjects of career and ministry. So many people are unclear about how to find their place of work in God's kingdom. But it's not so hard. The authors in this chapter found their life's work simply by following God each day. They did not have full knowledge of a master plan. They just believed God, picked up where they were, and did the things God put before them to do. Day by day they found that doing what God wanted them to do *was* the Master's plan.

I like to think of God's work as being like church handbells at Christmastime. Thirty single handbells, all sized to different pitches, lie silent on a table. Then the music starts, and the players ring the right bell at just the right moment in the musical score. If a player were to stand up and play his or her bell alone, it wouldn't sound like anything. But as all the players work together under the direction of the conductor, it's beautiful music.

There's a certain personality type in business that gets the job done. You know the kind. They work the long hours; they travel; they teach. They work within a team framework to achieve their objectives, and they never, ever give up. Henry Blackaby is that kind of man. Here he describes what fills the hours in the life he's turned over to God.

Henry Blackaby

Every day I get up very early to spend several hours in God's Word and in prayer. I'm very sensitive about being in absolute harmony with what God is up to in my day. Then I watch to see what God is doing as I proceed through the day.

My wife asked me, "What are you doing today?" I said, "I just counted up, and between this weekend and the middle of August I'll speak fifty-nine times. I have to prepare and prepare thoroughly." Each of those engagements is quite different. What I'll be doing in Europe is different than what I'll be doing at our conference center in New Mexico, which is different than what I'll be doing with a group of leaders in Florida and at a conference in Alaska.

So day in and day out, my number one priority is watching to see what God is doing around me and then making sure I'm integrating what He is doing into my life. After I finish speaking with you, I'll be speaking to a group of CEOs of Fortune 500 companies who want deeply to be witnesses for Christ in the marketplace where they are. Then at 6:30 tomorrow morning, I'll do a Bible study called "God in the Workplace" for about one hundred people from the business community. I've been doing that study once a month for a couple of years.

I'm trying, in the midst of everything else, to do some writing. I just completed a work on how God shapes the man He calls His friend, which is a study on the life of Abraham. I'm in the process of doing a book with my older son on spiritual leadership, and one with a pastor on revival, and one with a leader at the Sunday School Board on the ways of God. Between my family commitments, my assignment at the North American Mission Board, the other agencies I'm involved with, and my own sense of commitment to the Lord, my days are full. But they always begin with an unhurried time in the presence of God.

———

What makes a writer want to write? Running deep inside the veins of writers are the very experiences that make them want to write in the first place. Sheila Walsh confesses that her 1996 book, Honestly, *which dealt with her struggle with depression, was not originally intended for public consumption. She wrote it for herself—for the purpose of remembering. But through her gift of writing, her courageous testimony has given hope to thousands of others with similar struggles.*

Sheila Walsh

I didn't write *Honestly* as something I intended for publication. I just didn't want to forget a single moment of what I now consider to be one of the greatest adventures of my life. Of course, it didn't seem like a great adventure at the time. When you find yourself on the *700 Club* as Pat Robertson's co-host one morning and locked in a psychiatric hospital ward by that evening—that doesn't seem like good news!

But I realized something very simple that to me was profound. Some of God's most precious gifts come in packages that make our hands bleed when we open them. I realized that what I had been longing for all my life was a personal, face-to-face, intimate relationship with Christ based on nothing that I had to bring—because nothing I could bring would ever be enough. I had lived my life feeling that I was just four cents short of a dollar. But at that moment when I had nothing left, when I could have lain down in the ashes of my life, I never felt more embraced by God. I found what I had been looking for all my life.

———

As a writer myself, it's fascinating for me to explore how other writers approach their craft. Some are highly disciplined; others prefer to create as the mood strikes them. I asked Frank Peretti how he goes about the task of making a novel come to life.

Frank Peretti

I'm an everyday, so-many-hours writer, because the mood very seldom strikes me. I like to write, of course, but I can't sit around waiting for inspiration to hit. For me, writing is what Edison said: 1 percent inspiration and 99 percent perspiration. It's work. You just have to sit down and do it. So at about ten o'clock every morning I set a kitchen timer for five hours, I hit the button, and I start working. When I have to get up to answer the door or talk on the phone or go get the mail—there are a zillion different things that can distract you, and I can find any one of them at any time—I stop the clock, and I do whatever I have to do. Then I come back and start it again. That way I have some kind of discipline to make sure that I actually put in five real hours of writing. It doesn't always work, let me tell you. Sometimes it can be getting near bedtime and I've still got two hours left on the clock—and I don't know where the time went.

When I finally finish a book, Barb and I always go out to dinner or something. After I've worked—and I've worked on some of my books for two years—we're ready to celebrate!

Frank's books often have a spiritual warfare theme. I asked him: Is this because of a personal interest or because it's a great dramatic device?

I think it's a split down the middle. On the one hand, I have a fascination with spiritual warfare; on the other hand, it's something the readers have come to expect. If it's a Peretti novel, it's going to have to deal in some way with bridging the natural and the supernatural world. I think spiritual warfare is a really good device; it makes a story intriguing, so I don't mind going there. Besides, I'm writing primarily for Christians. The supernatural is not a problem; people can accept it. And it has dramatic power. It's a good venue for telling a story.

———

The ability to create stories that fascinate and inspire readers is a gift. But where does that gift come from? Max Lucado explains how he understands the awesome creative gift God has given him.

Max Lucado

I remember reading a quote in which one man announced, "I'm going to take a course in creative writing," and another guy said, "Is there any other kind?" I think that's pretty good! I've never set out saying, "I'm going to be creative." That's just what flows out of me. I don't even find it to be that creative!

You can tell when someone has a gift. Michael Card would say, "You know, playing thirteen-thousand instruments and writing songs and having an understanding of theology—that's not so hard." Well, it is to the rest of us! But he's got a gift, a spiritual anointing in those areas. I walk into our bookkeeper's office, and I don't see how she does what she does—but she does it with relative ease. That's the sign. You know you have a gift when people say, "How do you do that?" I think God said, "I'm going to give Max a gift of writing, communicating, and speaking. I don't know if I can trust Him with much more." He didn't entrust me with a good golf swing, I know that!

lessons for a broader audience

Actually, I've never known if I'm a minister who writes or a writer who ministers. I hope I never have to choose between the two. All of my messages, with the exception of the children's books I write, come out of lessons that I prepare for our church. When I'm preparing my lessons, hopefully I'm doing so under God's guidance. I say, "What does our church need to hear?" The assumption I make is that what the church needs to hear would be appreciated by a broader audience.

Not everything that's preached is eventually published. On Sundays after a service I know if the message I preached worked; I know if it connected with the people. I can tell by the looks on their faces and by the way they talk to me afterward. I know if that message passed the test.

We tape the messages, but we don't simply transcribe them. I do a lot of work on them to get them ready for publication. We've counted: From the time a message is preached to the time it's published, it goes through at least forty-five revisions. A lot of working and reworking is necessary because the eye and the ear are two different tools. You can't be too poetic with the ear, because it doesn't hear as fast as you can speak; it doesn't keep up with the voice. But with the eye you can be more creative, because the eye can control the pace of the reception of the message.

a different kind of minister

Fortunately, I have a really great work situation here at the church. I'm senior minister in a church of about 2700 people. But my role is very different than any other senior minister I know of. We have an executive minister on staff, and he really does everything a senior minister does except preach. He's very good—an exceptionally good manager. He runs the staff of about thirty-five people. We have a nice facility and there's a lot to do, but I don't have to do what he does.

I don't draw a salary from the church. I did for the first two years I was here, but then I went to the elders and said, "If I can have more of a writing and preaching role, you can have my salary to bring in an administrator." So that's what happened. I have the title of senior minister, and most people think, "That means he's in charge of everything." But the truth is, I know very little. I only have a key to get into my own office, and I'm very happy not to have any others. The less I can do, the better!

———

As laypeople, we often don't recognize the full measure of the responsibilities carried out by the pastoral staff at church. Scotty Smith reveals what he sees as his calling as a pastor and where he gets the passion to do what he does.

Scotty Smith

Passion is simply the energy, the creativity, the gifts, the heart, the longings that God has given us released in some direction. The centering of passion happened for me, and continues to happen for me, as I am astonished at the good news of what God has done for us in Christ. My core passion is bound up with the gospel. Jesus Christ has come into this world. He is full of grace and truth. The packaging, the releasing, the disseminating of that passion—that's up to God and His sovereign purposes. It just so happens that in His sense of humor, He made me a pastor, which is something I never chose to be!

As senior pastor at Christ Community Church, my calling is in three areas: vision casting, the ministry of the Word, and helping to structure and implement a lifestyle of worship. Christ Community has a commitment to become a worshiping community. I work very closely with the director of our worship ministry to help structure a worship environment in which the gospel will flourish.

But my main calling as senior pastor is to have vision—long-term and short-term—for the church. It's my calling to interpret for the body what I sense God is calling Christ Community Church to do in the work of the kingdom and in the greater middle Tennessee area, along with the other outstanding churches around us. What is our calling? Where do we fit in with what God is doing with, through, and in other fellowships?

———

Patsy Clairmont overcame many obstacles on her journey to becoming a great writer. For Patsy, it all began with a dream placed in her heart since childhood and a love of words.

Patsy Clairmont

I've always loved words. I love Scrabble, I love crossword puzzles, I love when words line up and marry and say something so sweet and dear. I just love words! I have a natural heart for words— which is what my first editor told me. She listened to some of my speaking tapes and said, "I have listened to how you speak, and this is what I know about you: Putting aside your educational deficiencies, you love words. That's the most important ingredient we could work with." And so it was through her ear, her very understanding and patient heart, and her direction that I learned how to do what I had wanted to do since I was a little girl.

One of the most significant factors affecting our work is who we work with. I asked Patsy to share what it's like working alongside some of the well-known and respected speakers of the popular Women of Faith conferences.

A tremendous amount of laughter takes place because these are really funny women. They're very spontaneous with their humor, so at any given point we may be in gales of laughter. After we've been intensely involved in ministry, laughter is a way of unwinding. We really give out so much, which is our calling; but after we've given out for a weekend, and we've been with thousands of women, we enjoy just being together in a small group, appreciating the fact that God designed us to laugh until we cry. He knew that both laughing and crying would give us release and relief. We can get kind of silly once in a while, and we enjoy the silliness.

We interact at different levels because some of these gals have been friends much longer than others. For instance, Marilyn Meberg and Luci Swindoll have been friends for twenty-five years, whereas I have only known Marilyn since the conferences started a few years ago. So there are different levels of friendship. Sheila Walsh was new to all of us. We all had heard of her ministry, but we had not met her personally. She fit in our system like a glove—a kindred sister.

In 1996 attendance at Women of Faith conferences peaked at 30,000 attendees. By 1998 attendance had surpassed 350,000 with events in twenty-eight cities. No one could have predicted that sports arenas would fill to capacity with women who wanted to take part in these unique events, yet that's exactly what happened! I asked conference speaker Barbara Johnson to explain their phenomenal popularity.

Barbara Johnson

I think there are a lot of hurting women out there, and they need a message of love, encouragement, and hope. The flavor of each of us who speak is different. One of us speaks mostly about everlasting love, one speaks about instilling hope in parents, and another gives a story of encouragement. So each one has a little finger in there, and one of those fingers is going to minister to each of the ladies in attendance. There isn't one woman who will come to a conference and not hear something that will touch her heart.

I just see God using this. It's been phenomenal. The first year we held the conferences in churches; the second year we started holding them in arenas. They said we were going to be at the Anaheim Pond, which holds 22,000, and I thought that was a joke—we never could do that. But we filled that arena three times to capacity, with 2,000 overflowing. My gift of joy may have helped, but my faith sure didn't!

I really think we're heading toward revival. I work with thousands of women; women read my books, and I read letters from them. I feel that women's hearts are being touched by the message of encouragement we share through Women of Faith. The salvation message is always given. Marilyn Meberg presents the gospel, Campus Crusade follows up, and we always get all the notes from the women who accept the Lord, who say they have a new direction in their lives. We read all these comments, and it's rewarding for us to see what these women say the conference has done for them.

So I think God's hand is on what we're doing. I don't really know why, because we all are very ordinary, down-to-earth women. I am. I answer my own phone, flush my own toilet, don't have a maid, and I live in a mobile home. How can you be more normal and down-to-earth than that? Even though we come from a variety of backgrounds, all of us are pretty much the same. None of us came from a really wealthy background; none of us are overly educated. Yet God has taken these women and used their stories so that the flavor that comes through is God's love, and that love is touching people's hearts.

—

If you haven't heard him speak, Steve Brown has an incredible broadcaster's voice. He started out working in radio, as Steve puts it, before "Jesus became real to me." This is a fascinating story about how the radio profession that Steve loved was taken away from him—only to return in a way he least expected.

Steve Brown

My background is in commercial broadcasting. When I was in college and later on in Boston, I was a morning man and then a newsman and production manager. I was so sure when Jesus became real to me that God would, of course, use me in broadcasting, because I had these wonderful gifts. But God said, "I was doing fine before you came along; I don't need you." So for twenty-five years I went in a different direction, and I assumed that my broadcasting days were over. You know, once you're bitten by the radio bug, it really gets to you. It's really fun stuff to do. But I had to put it on the altar.

just what the world needs

At Key Biscayne in Miami our church had a tape ministry like many churches do; we recorded the sermons and if people wanted tapes, they could get them at a nominal cost. At some point a Jewish friend of mine who is a believer, Eddie Waxer, said, "You ought to make those tapes free." I said, "You're crazy. If I give them away for free, I will go broke." But he responded, "I'll put twenty thousand dollars in the bank. You make them free."

Because I'd written some books, I was traveling and speaking a lot. Sometimes I'd put a legal pad on a table where I was speaking and tell people they could write down their names and addresses if they wanted tapes. We sent out about 350,000 tapes a year that way. Then another friend of mine who was managing five radio stations decided to record an opening and closing on the tapes and started broadcasting them without asking my permission. An agency got involved, and the messages were tested on twelve stations.

I told the agency at the time, "That is just what the world needs, another Bible teacher on the radio. It's not as if we don't have the best in the country on the air already!" But I think maybe there are people out there who screw up a lot like me, and they need somebody like that on the radio too. I think it was Moody who said, "We don't want a bunch of you, but I'm glad there's one."

We were told that we'd probably get 150 letters from listeners the first month. Well, we got 3,000 letters. One of the guys said, "They are writing us like we are some big ministry, and there's just you and me!" Needless to say, we were pleased and surprised with the response, but we had to play catch-up real fast.

the gift of a great voice

These days I do a show every morning in Tampa and St. Petersburg, and also in Savannah and Atlanta. It's kind of an in-your-face, comedic, political, serious, not-so-serious, three-hour program. Once a guy called me up and said, "Steve, you're enamored with your own voice." And I said, "Of course I am. If you were as ugly as I am and had a voice as good as mine, you would be too." People are always saying that when they hear me on radio, they expect to meet a Marlboro Man in person. They are always horribly disappointed. I didn't do anything to get this voice. I mean, I've never been trained.

I didn't do elocution lessons or anything like that. My mother said I sounded like a burp when I came out of the womb. It's sort of like grace: You don't do anything to earn it, it just *is*.

———

By now, we've all heard about the mysterious Bible codes—the highly controversial discovery that by searching through the Hebrew Bible text, circling a certain letter, and then skipping a specific number of letters, names and events that occur at a future date are spelled out. Many skeptics doubt the validity of the Bible codes, and as the author of this book, I need to state clearly that I am one of those skeptics. However, when I sat across from Grant Jeffrey in his home in Toronto, I wanted to know how he came to write about the codes and why he believes they are credible.

Grant Jeffrey

Twelve years ago I was reading an Israeli newspaper in Jerusalem when I noticed a little side paragraph that said that Israeli scientists had discovered through computer biolinguistic analysis that the book of Genesis had one author, not five. Now, the documentary hypothesis that has been popular for one hundred years in seminaries is that because Genesis uses several different names for God—Adonai and so on—there were five different authors, and an editor put it together. What the newspaper article said, however, was that there was something running through every one of the passages in Genesis that indicated one mind. I thought that was fascinating at the time.

A year or two later I came to understand that the scientists had actually found a series of codes. Naturally I was very, very skeptical.

I was concerned that the idea of a Bible code would be found to be frivolous—that it was something that wasn't real or something that could be used by people who have no sense of the value of inspirational Scripture. However, as I continued to research and talk to my friends who were rabbis, I began to realize that some very serious people had looked into this idea and believed it was for real.

For about ten years I slowly gathered information about the codes, at first through secondhand sources and later firsthand. I did not write about them, although at that time I was writing several books in which it would have been very easy to include something about the codes. But I had yet to be utterly certain in my own spirit that the discovery was of God; that it would honor the Word of God; that it had nothing to do with numerology; that it did not violate God's law against fortunetelling and trying to predict future events; and lastly, that it lifted up Jesus Christ.

looking for the seal of approval

I acquired the computer programs that were used to study the Bible codes on our trip to Israel in the early 1990s. In fact, it was during the Gulf War, the last day before the first scud missiles hit Israel. My wife, Kay, and I were in Jerusalem, and while everyone was going around with gas masks waiting for the missiles to hit, I went down to an old Jewish rabbinical bookstore and acquired the computer programs that I had been reading and hearing about. I began to do the experiments myself, and that's when I verified that the code phenomenon was absolutely real. I also verified that it dealt with Jesus. That was, to me, the ultimate seal of the approval of God. The codes lifted up the name of Jesus and identified Him as the Messiah repeatedly. It was Yacov Rambsel who first discovered this about the name of Jesus, and once he told me what he'd found, I was able to verify it myself with the computer.

the first five hours

When I first got the programs home and got them into my computer, I spent about five hours looking for biblical words. I looked for Abraham; I looked for Isaac. And it was fascinating, because their names turned up in code in places where they appeared in the surface text. Interestingly, the Israelis had done an experiment in which they found the names Hitler, Eichmann, the word *holocaust*, and the names of the death camps, and I was able to verify them. I could see them with my own eyes.

Of course, I was not willing to trust the computer program alone. I then went to the Hebrew-English Interlinear Bible, the very large volume edited by Jay Green Sr. that most pastors use in seminaries. I went to the particular passages and began highlighting them in yellow and verifying that, yes, these things were there in the Masoretic text used by Jews throughout the world. Without any modifications to the text, these codes were there.

I understand why many people are skeptical about this, as I was. I waited ten years before I was willing to write about the Bible codes because it is such an astonishing discovery. It's so strange. That's why I've explicitly explained in my books, *The Handwriting of God* and *The Signature of God*, that the codes have nothing to do with numerology. It's irrelevant what number is skipped; the important thing is whether there's a meaningful word that is found, and then not just one word, but a group of words, a cluster of words in a small area. This also has nothing to do with fortunetelling. You can't predict events. It's only after an event occurs that you know the details and can look for them. The names Eichmann, Hitler, holocaust—you can look for them now, after the fact. The Bible codes are an apologetic device. They act as evidence of the supernatural origin of the Bible, because no human could possibly have encoded such information into the text.

a generation without excuse

Jay Green Sr., the editor of the Hebrew-English Interlinear Bible, did a book review of *The Signature of God*. He looked at the Bible codes with the same consternation as I did at first, but he has verified that all the codes are there and has stated so in writing. Some brilliant Israeli scientists and mathematicians, together with David Kazhdan, the head of mathematics at Harvard University, have examined the codes scientifically and have stated that there is a real phenomenon at work here that is not found in other texts.

The critics of the Bible code phenomenon have made some erroneous statements on the Internet, saying that you can find the same kind of thing at work in Tolstoy's *War and Peace* and Melville's *Moby Dick*. But they're not finding the same phenomenon at all. They're finding an incredibly diminished thing; they find one encoded word at some great interval and then a word in the surface text, and they say, "See, this is like the Bible codes." No, with the Bible codes we find multiple words—say, thirteen words or more encoded within two paragraphs—and they're about something that would have been in the future. That's the kind of thing we have challenged our critics to find in any text in the world—Hebrew, English, anything outside the Bible. They simply can't.

I mean, we found forty-one names in Isaiah 53—the names of Jesus and His disciples and other historical characters. This is something that is unprecedented and not found in other texts. I really believe the Bible code phenomenon is a tremendous apologetic device that speaks uniquely to our computer-literate generation. I think it's the last measure of evidence needed so that our generation is really without excuse.

———

Karyn Henley was already writing professionally when she got the idea for The Beginners Bible—*a response to her need for a Bible that the young children in her own home could understand. Since its publication, the book has been translated into seventeen languages and has sold more than three million copies, proving that inventive solutions to common problems can be universal in their appeal.*

Karyn Henley

I began writing Bible stories sometime after my first son was born in 1979. As we did our devotional time, I would try to read the Bible to my son. I would automatically change the words as I went along so he could understand; and having worked with young children, I was familiar with doing that. Then I began to look for Bible storybooks that had stories for him at his level, and I would try to read them. But they'd have an entire page that was a beautiful picture and an entire page of text. They really weren't written for the preschooler; they were for an older child.

So I began writing stories that had pictures. In fact I drew the first pictures for what eventually began *The Beginners Bible*. I would draw the pictures with a marker, and then I'd place along the bottom some very simple words that had to do with the Bible story and the picture. I would use several pictures for a very short story, and that seemed to hold my son's attention best.

About that time I ordered some paperback books and tapes from a secular company with traditional stories that we all tell our kids. My son enjoyed those so much that I said, "Why can't we do something like this in the Christian market, with Bible stories instead of secular ones?" That was my vision: to have a set of paperback books with tapes. When a friend who was doing marketing through Christian schools called and asked me if we had any resources that he could use, we said, "We do have an idea for a set of books and tapes. Would that be something you would like to market to your schools?" He answered, "I think that would work great!" So from that came a set of books and tapes called *Dove Tales,* which eventually were compiled into what we know now as *The Beginners Bible.*

As a mom, I knew there was a need for something like that. If you are a writer, when you see there is a need in the market, you look to write something that fills that need. You say, Where is the niche? Where is the need? What is missing here? You try to go for that, if you are wise. Sometimes you write something and just place it out there in the middle of a lot of competition, because you just feel that you've got something that's really good. But in the case of *The Beginners Bible,* there turned out to be a niche and a need that other parents obviously felt too. It surprised me; I knew there was a need, but I had no idea it was so deep.

And the need is international. One day a man approached me with the idea of coming to New Zealand to talk to teachers and parents about communicating with children. He did not know at that time that I already did this in the U.S., that I traveled with seminars for teachers and parents. So in the spring of 1995 we spent four or five weeks in New Zealand, doing seminars and concerts for children and parents. Since then we've gone to Russia and taught in the area of writing for children; specifically, writing Sunday school materials. In a couple of weeks we will be going to England, where I will be holding a parenting seminar. We will be talking to people there about revival and about how I might be involved in some of their efforts. We will be going to New Zealand again for about a week, and then we will be in Australia for another five weeks, taking our information over there, holding concerts, and talking to parents about communicating with children. Wherever we go, everything we do is about communication—enabling and equipping parents and teachers to communicate effectively with children, wherever they live.

———◆———

In his best-selling book, Connecting, *Larry Crabb writes about the changes that have taken place in his work in recent years. A licensed psychotherapist, counselor, and professor of graduate studies at Colorado Christian University, his interests have turned to personal relationships within the church and how we can utilize those relationships to make us more like Christ.*

Larry Crabb

I've had so many interesting responses to *Connecting*. Some of my students from fifteen, sixteen, seventeen years ago read the book and say, "You've been saying this all along." But I say, "No, this is a big step for me. How dare you say I've been saying this all along!"

Now my effort is to take the idea of *Connecting* further. My book after *Connecting* is called *The Safest Place on Earth*, and it's a sequel to *Connecting*. It says that a connecting community is the safest place on earth for the Spirit to do His work, and it's the most dangerous place on earth for the flesh to continue its work. That's the theme of the new book. It's the next step.

I'm not sure what I'm doing here, but I know this: Way down deep, I've always felt that this whole thing called counseling or psychotherapy is fundamentally a spiritual enterprise. It's fundamentally dealing with spiritual issues, because the root of all the stuff we call psychological or emotional really has to do with matters of the soul. It's never made great sense to me to think that the person who can deal with me best when I'm struggling is somebody who's academically trained and therefore has a handbag full of techniques and verbal strategies and all that. What I need, what I long for in my soul, is to have somebody pour out of themselves what's most alive in them, and in that process ignite what's most alive in me as a believer. That doesn't feel like psychotherapy to me; that feels like a distinctly spiritual enterprise.

My feeling is that if we as believers are going to work with others who are struggling with anorexia, bulimia, multiple personalities, depression, anxiety attacks—all the stuff we label as psychological disorders and refer to professionals—our need isn't so much for academic training in theory and technique. Rather, we need to be willing to move into their lives and together experience the deeper reality of the Spirit within us. When we know that a miracle really has taken place in the regenerate heart, and when that miracle evidences itself in what comes out of us and goes into somebody else, then I believe the real work of healing takes place.

when words aren't enough

This is such a huge concept, and I feel as if my words are feeble. Back in the old days when I was able to draw wonderful charts on blackboards and overhead projectors, people would say, "Oh, now I see what you're talking about." But I feel as if I was wrapping my mind around small topics back then. Now that I'm trying to put words to a very big topic, I'm having trouble. When I do public speaking, I think that audiences leave with all sorts of things. But I think as a general theme, people leave saying, "There's something here. I don't quite know what it means, and I don't quite know how to get there; but I think it's wonderful, I think it's central—and I don't know what to do about it."

Connecting is the most thoroughly unmanageable element in life. We're determined to manage life, however, so we take on only that version of Christianity that we can manage. We can manage orchestrating a wonderful church service. We can get a worship leader to pick the right music, and we can get the pastor to have his sermon match the worship. I'm not faulting that kind of effort; I don't think it's wrong to manage what can be managed. But I think the error is in saying that what is manageable, what is legitimately manageable, is the priority, the first thing. C. S. Lewis has a wonderful quote in which he says that when we live for first things, second things are thrown in. Live for second things, and you lose both first and second things. I believe we're settling for second things that are legitimately good; but when second things become first, everything gets messed up.

living for congeniality, not connection

When we connect, we introduce conflict; as soon as we make an effort to connect, we get uncomfortable. We get out of our comfort zone and into a sphere requiring radical dependence on God. I think that's why most of us approach church as a country club: We've decided we're going to handle conflict by staying congenial.

Frankly, most of us don't connect; instead, we live for congeniality, cooperation, or consolation. Congeniality is: "Let's have a neighborhood barbecue." Cooperation is: "Let's work together to make our schools more safe." Consolation is: "My gosh, you're really hurting; let me give you a hug. I know things are tough; I'll buy you dinner." The reason we live for congeniality, cooperation, or consolation is because we haven't found the answer to conflict. We haven't found the answer to the fact that when you and I get to know each other really well, I'm not going to like you very much, and you're not going to like me. There's stuff about me that's ugly!

The only way for us to get along at the deepest level is through the gospel, through a radical dependence on the New Covenant. That requires too much of us, however, so we settle for sociability, congeniality. We settle for working together on a good project. If a loved one dies, we settle for a card and a nice hug and a word of prayer, and we get on with our lives.

a deeper passion

I live ten minutes away from Littleton, Colorado, where the Columbine High School shootings took place in 1999. In the aftermath of that event we all talked about violence in the schools, gun control legislation, and so on. That's fine; I'm sure there are a lot of things that need to be done to prevent similar tragedies. But we also saw an outpouring of connection in these parts that was staggering.

Is connecting going to solve the problem? No, I think it's utopian to assume we're going to solve all the problems in the world. But it's not utopian to assume that if I could find a handful of people and pour my life into them, and if a couple of people would pour their lives into me, we'd begin to experience a filling of that deficit in our souls that would make pornography and suicide and affairs and divorce and all the rest less attractive. Somebody has said that the only way we're going to solve crimes of passion—and all sin is fundamentally passionate—is to nudge them aside with a deeper passion.

What's the Secret?

The calling to which we dedicate our lives should be a labor of love. How do we find that calling? We ask God. Then we can rest assured that whatever field we're in, God will show us how we can serve Him—in faith expressing itself through love—right where we are.

Secret #5

Perfect Love
Can't Give Us Second Best

Summertime will always be the first thing I picture when I think of happiness. Growing up in the cold-weather state of Michigan, I cherished those short summer months when the daylight lasted a little longer and the sun thawed out the frozen memories of the long, harsh winter. Summertime skies always seemed a little brighter, more vivid, as if the colors had just migrated back from some warm and exotic locale where they'd spent the winter.

I still love summer. It's a time for lazy afternoons reading in a hammock, driving around with the windows rolled down and the radio on, backyard chats with the neighbors, trips downtown for ice cream, going for a swim in the pool. It's a time for fresh strawberries, ripe watermelon, and cool, juicy plums bought at the farmer's roadside stand. It's a time for pickup basketball games with the guys, nature walks with the family, and mid-Saturday afternoon naps (and waking to find it's still bright outside!) Some of the all-time greatest smells occur only in summertime: freshly cut grass, steaks on the grill, coconut suntan lotion. And the arrival of summer always means it's time to take a vacation, preferably to a favorite Florida beach: Daytona, Destin, Ormond.

I wonder if in these simple summer pleasures, God is speaking to me in a language He knows I can understand. Sometimes all the intricacies of theology get simplified—reduced down to something I can almost touch with my fingertips and hold within the palms of my hands. And that something is this: God loves us and has our best interests in mind. Or as Henry Blackaby says, "Perfect love can't give us second best."

I think I'm getting a handle on God's goodness, not just because I've read about it in the Bible, but because I've experienced it in my own life. God is the creator of this good earth. The wonderful moments we enjoy in summertime (and in other seasons as well) are there because He's made them for us. He has our best interests at heart, and He gives us good gifts. Of course, with those gifts He also gives us boundaries; but if we are wise, we understand that His precepts aren't meant to keep us from having a life but to make life possible.

God's love is amazing and unsearchable in its completeness. The story of our lives is the story of His great love for us, His plans to bless and not harm us, and His desire to adopt us into His family. Our role is simply to believe in Him, to trust and obey. Perfect love is easy in His hands but impossible in ours, so He tells us to trust Him. Any further directive is unnecessary. If we begin to feel lost in this sometimes confusing world, we need only to return to His simple instructions: "Follow Me." We can be sure that Jesus is heading in the right direction because He *is* the right direction.

Each of us longs to know that God is good and that He truly

loves us. That's the reason I have made it my work to collect contemporary stories of personal faith from our leaders and our peers. Stories renew and rekindle our faith in God. They spark wonder as we gaze into each other's lives and see how real God is. They allow us to see what we might not see without someone's example. They remind us that God hasn't stopped doing miracles; He hasn't stopped listening to prayers. Stories tell us that God loves us, and they assure us that He's willing to forgive us for our (many) blunders.

God continually reaches out His open hand to us. His constant plea is that we turn from our wicked ways and believe in Him. He continually challenges us to surrender these broken lives we're living, lives that haven't worked without Him anyway, and to trust Christ. When we see what He has done in the lives of others—whether they are men and women from the Bible or contemporary Christians we know and respect—we gain the courage to step out in faith, believing that His love will be there for us too.

This is a chapter about the love of God. It tells stories of healings, transformations, and heart surgeries, both literal and figurative. It tells of prayers that are answered, joy that is found in the midst of suffering, and the sufficiency of God's grace in all situations.

For the authors I interviewed, God's love is an ever-present fact of life. Here, as they tell of their gratitude for His many blessings, they express an intimacy with Christ that only comes from having laid one's head upon the chest of Jesus. I started out by asking the authors how they first came to believe that God loves them. I wanted to know how they experienced the love of God in their lives. In their answers I heard a settledness. I heard a calmness of voice that comes only when we know what we know.

I couldn't help but wonder, *Does my voice have that same calmness?*

Does yours? How has God revealed His love to you? As we read the stories that follow, let's think about our own stories too. And let's take comfort in the knowledge that God knows each one of us; He knows how unique we are. And He knows how to speak to us in just the way we will understand.

We will never know everything there is to know about God. The depths of His love for us, the full meaning of the cross, and the splendor of His grace are impervious mysteries to our human minds. Every once in a while, though, we get a clearer glimpse and a closer view.

Sheila Walsh

When I look out across the Christian landscape, I see a tremendous human struggle to fully understand the gospel; and yet I imagine that 98 percent of us haven't even begun to grasp what Christianity is really all about. To me the cross is a prime symbol of the fact that nothing we could do would ever be enough. The fact that Christ took all our shame on Himself—all the garbage that Sheila Walsh ever did and will ever do—says as clearly as anything could: "You're never going to make it by yourself. I've seen your struggles, I've seen your effort. I've seen everything you've tried to do, and it won't ever be enough. So I am going to take your place."

We accept that, and then we think, *Here is this outrageous free gift; now what can I do to earn it?* We go out of our way to try to make ourselves worthy of the gift that God has already given! Then we struggle because we feel as if we are two different people. Paul talked about this when he said, "I'm a miserable man, because the thing I really want to do, I don't do; and the thing I don't want to do, I do."

You know, it is very common to the human condition, but the American church in the twentieth century is obsessed with success and appearance. We equate big numbers with God's blessing. We equate financial success with the approval of God. We've become very twisted in our understanding of the grace of God.

Let me tell you about grace. The end of the book of Malachi is followed by four hundred years of silence. Then God chooses to show up in the most glorious, unprecedented way, and it's not to the people you would imagine he would show up to. It's not to the impressive people in town, the people you want to hang with, or the people who can get things done. God shows up to the night shift, to the boys on the hill.

When I tell this story to women in conferences, I say, "You're so used to hearing the story of the messenger of God appearing to shepherds on the hillside that you forget how outrageous that is. So let me put it in a different context. Imagine that it is one minute to midnight. Stella and her cleaning crew at the local hospital are getting ready to put out their cigarettes, fill their buckets with hot, soapy water, and mop the corridors. Their hearts and minds are full of worries. Stella is worried about her husband because he is drinking again. Another woman is worried because she's sure her teenage daughter is sleeping with her boyfriend. Each of the women face private struggles that seem bigger than themselves.

"Suddenly a loud noise comes from the end of the corridor. It seems to be emanating from the operating room, which should be empty at this time of night. They grab their mops (insufficient weapons if something bad were really happening!), hurry to the end of the hallway, and open the door. There stands the most glorious sight Stella has ever seen in her long, hard life. With a wingspan of a thousand eagles, a messenger from God says, 'Stella, to you is born this day a Savior, who is Christ the Lord. To you, with your PMS and your varicose veins and your bag full of worries, to you is born a Savior!'"

I think this is the most radical way that God could have shown up—not to the religious leaders of the time, not to someone sitting on a throne, but to ordinary men and women carrying with them the burdens of life; and saying to these ordinary people, "To you is born a Savior." The word *savior* doesn't only mean someone who is going to rescue us; it means someone who is going to save us *and* heal us. We're saved in that moment we first respond to God; but then we begin a process that continues for the rest of our lives of being slowly healed by the love of God.

———

Something incredible and indestructible happens when we encounter God when there's nowhere else to turn. For the desperate who turn to the Lord and find Him, theirs is a faith built on a foundation of stone.

Steve Brown

I'm not from a particularly religious family. My father was a drunk. My mother read Spurgeon in the morning and the Bible at night, but she taught me how to cuss in between. There was never any pressure on me to go into the ministry. Yet from my earliest memories, I knew what I was going to do. When other kids were going to be cowboys, I was going to be a preacher. That has always been so, and I don't know where it came from except from God. I think God realized that I would run if He didn't make my calling clear very early.

Now, if you don't believe in God and you're going to be a preacher, you've got a serious problem! It's like me selling a hair restorer—and I'm quite bald, by the way. It just doesn't work. I did go forward in a Billy Graham crusade when I was sixteen, but after that I became an agnostic—you know, the stereotypical college agnostic with a major in philosophy. I went to Boston University School of Theology because you didn't have to believe anything and you could still become a reverend. I did the social ethics thing, and I was Steve Brown, boy psychologist.

Later, when I was a pastor on Cape Cod, our second daughter was born. She was very, very sick. She had a leg that the doctors called "maudlin." It wasn't getting nourishment. So they called in a specialist who said he had never seen a leg like that in twenty years of practice. She had a blood count that was elevating dangerously, and the doctor said that if it kept going up she would have to go to a children's hospital in Boston. Now, I wasn't a good person; but I did love my family, and I was devastated. She was only one day old!

Two weeks earlier I had met some Anglican charismatics. I'm not charismatic, but they were the only people I knew at the time who knew God. I'd have gone to a witch doctor if I'd known one. That night I explained to them that my daughter had been born, but she had some serious problems. So they joined hands and prayed for her. The next morning my wife called from the hospital and said, "Honey, did anybody pray last night?" I told her that the Anglicans did. And she proceeded to tell me that the doctor had come in that morning and said, "This is miraculous. Your daughter's blood count is normal, and we are no longer worried about the leg."

Now I'd presided over funerals and buried babies for couples who really knew God and loved Him. I didn't know Him or love Him. These people were a lot better than I was, yet their babies died and mine didn't. I didn't understand. I'd like to say that I fell on my knees at that moment and became a spiritual giant. But it took me about six years to come to a place of real faith because I had a lot of stuff in me, a lot of doubts. At least I knew at that point that God was there and that on at least one occasion, He had intervened in my life in a specific way. I was extremely grateful, but I didn't understand the details. I had written "inconsistent" on a lot of the pages of my Bible.

After a six-year period of much study and much trial, and with the help of some Christian brothers who loved me, I finally knelt down by my desk. By then I was serving a church in Boston, and I said, "God, I'm not good, but I'm yours. From now on the Bible will be my authority."

Incidentally, Steve's daughter is doing wonderfully now. She is healthy, loves Christ, and is married to a doctor in Birmingham, Alabama, with two daughters of her own.

———

Obviously, Steve Brown witnessed a miracle. Have you ever said to yourself, "If I could just see a miracle, then I wouldn't have all these doubts?" There's something to be said for trusting

God without needing to witness special, supernatural events. Yet God, by His very nature, is so miraculous that even His small acts have the ability to transform us. I asked Chonda Pierce if she'd ever seen a miracle.

Chonda Pierce

My son was born prematurely, and he was very, very sick. We started praying and got on the phone to tell our family members and friends to pray. The first ten hours are the key for preemies. If you can get them to that stage and then to the next stage, it's an uphill climb, but you know they'll make it.

For ten hours the doctors told us it could go either way. We thought, *God's either going to allow our son to live, or He's going to call him home.* We prayed, and it went our way. We praised the Lord for it. I remember feeling that I had seen a miracle.

I remember being a kid and praying in groceries. There were times when we sat down at suppertime with no food on the table, and we said grace anyway. Mama was such a believer! She'd say, "We're going to say grace, and the Lord's going to provide; and when we go to bed He's going to remove these hunger pains." And while we'd be praying, the doorbell would ring, and there would be somebody there with a bag of groceries! What a privilege it was to see this as a kid, because as a kid you know it is a God-thing.

I've seen things in my life in which I acknowledge the distinct hand of God. I get choked up saying it, but I acknowledge that His hand has been in my life from the first breath I ever breathed. That's the miracle—that God created me and He loves me. If I don't ever see another miracle, that one is it; that is enough. I have acknowledged Him. He forgives me of my sins and is taking me to heaven, so He doesn't have to do anything to prove Himself. He did it all on the cross for me.

I'm not in this Christian life to get what God's got. I'm in this just because I love Him. I've gotten to a place where I don't need to see signs and wonders. Now that's easy for me to say, because I don't have a child dying from a disease; I'm not facing a catastrophe that requires a miracle. But I can remember when my little sister was dying. I prayed really, really hard that she would be healed, and she wasn't. So I've had days when I've seen the signs of wonders, and I've had days when God didn't answer the way I wanted Him to. He's not a lottery ticket! My relationship with Him is much deeper than that.

———

Once in a great while I hear one of those stories that makes the hair on the back of my neck stand up. I asked Larry Crabb if he has ever experienced the Spirit of God directly. His story reminds us that while God's Spirit isn't visible, His presence can be as real as if He were standing right next to us.

Larry Crabb

God feels far more silent than talkative to me. I wish He were a little more loquacious! But there have been moments. I don't think my faith is based on the moments of supernatural or mystical experience; my faith is rooted in the fact that I believe God has spoken and the Bible is true. That's the foundation of my faith. But I'll tell you, if it weren't for a couple of mystical experiences, I'd be a dry, dry sponge.

There have been moments when *mysticism* has become a wonderful word for me. Six months ago I went to speak at a church. An hour of worship preceded my two-hour lecture that night, and at about a quarter till eight, I found myself praying. I was going to be speaking in fifteen minutes, but I was caught up in the worship, and I said, "Lord, if this 'connecting' stuff that I'm teaching about is from You, I just have to know it. You've got to let me know. If I've simply made it up because I have a fertile mind and now that I'm getting older I want something new to talk about, let me know so I can dump the whole thing. But if this is a message from You, I want to know it."

This is what I was praying silently to myself in the front row of the church. Then I said, "Lord, I'd love to know this weekend." That last line was just one of those weird little prayers that popped out of my heart and through my mouth. Within a few minutes of praying that prayer—I'd say at about ten till eight—some guy I'd never met before came up to the front row, stood next to me, and said, "Can I have a word with you?" My thought was, *This is a bad time. I'm going to be speaking in ten minutes to a thousand people, and I've been sitting here praying and worshiping and getting ready, and I don't want to talk to you right now.* But I'm more polite than that! I said, "Sure, what do you want?" He said, "I'm one of the pastors here, and ever since I knew you were coming to our church, I've been praying for you every day. I believe God wants me to say something to you."

Well, I'm not used to hearing that kind of thing, but he continued, "I sense that you're struggling with whether your message is from God or not. You really want to know, and you want to know this weekend. I'm here to tell you that you're going to know this weekend." I thought, *Holy Toledo! What is going on here?* That's the sort of stuff that ten years ago I would have debunked and called silly. But I don't believe it's silly. I've been confining the Spirit far too long.

That was an experience that led me to say, "Lord, there's something so real about You. Yet you're so confusing to me. Why couldn't You be real on schedule? Why couldn't You be real in the ways that I've prayed for that have gone unanswered? Why do You come through at a moment like *this?*" God is so unpredictable, so unmanageable, so untamable! But every now and then, He does something that makes me say, "My gosh, You're really there, and my life is in Your hands."

———

The Bible records occasions when Jesus did not perform miracles. Henry Blackaby explains that it was not that Jesus couldn't, but that He chose not to.

Henry Blackaby

The best thing that ever happened to me took place when I was a little boy: God convinced me that He is God and I'm not. I've never come into the presence of God without that deep understanding. This morning when I got up before God, I acknowledged that He is God and I'm not, and He has a sovereign right to do what He wants to.

He has not left us ignorant of His ways, however. The whole of Scripture is God-centered. The Bible reveals the nature of God. That means we can know ahead of time that there are some things God will never do and some things He will always do, because that's

His nature. He will never go contrary to His nature. Perfect love, for instance, cannot give us second best; God would have to cease to be God to respond to us with less than perfect love.

But the Bible also reveals the ways of God. It's not that God can't do something, it's that He chooses not to do something when His people are living in sin. In Isaiah 59 God says, "You need to know that my arm is not too short that it cannot save, nor my ear too heavy that it cannot hear; but your iniquity, your sin, has come between you and Me, so I choose not to." It's not that Jesus couldn't do mighty works because of unbelief, it's that He chose not to. Unbelief does not block the sovereignty of God, but it does determine the sovereignty of God in the sense that He has said, "Where I find unbelief, I'll choose not to work."

In my own life personally and in the churches I've pastored, I've recognized that if there was no evidence of God's mighty presence working through us, the problem was not with God; it was with us. I would immediately go to God and say, "Oh Lord, what is it about our walk with You that is causing You to choose not to bless us and work mightily through us?" Then I'd go to the Scriptures to seek a word from God. In John 8:31–32 He says, "If you remain in My word, then you are My disciples, and you will know the truth, and the truth will set you free."

When God's people are praying but nothing is happening, some throw up their hands and say, "Well, it's just the sovereignty of God." And I say, "No, no, no, no, no. It is the sovereignty of God, but we're not ignorant of the ways of God. If He chooses not to, it's because there's sin and rebellion in our hearts, so that He won't." As the psalmist says, "If I hold sin in my heart, God will not hear me."

The word *hear* means to listen and then respond immediately. It's not that He can't hear you or that He doesn't know what you're saying; it's that He chooses not to respond.

It is amazing to me that God has made known to His people all of His ways, all of His promises, all of His nature, and yet we don't take time to know what He's like or to know His ways. I cannot remember a time when God made Himself known to me in His nature or His ways, impacting me in such a way that I made an adjustment to God, that I did not soon see Him manifesting Himself that way in my life. My heart cry is, How can I help the people of God to understand the nature of God and the ways of God, identify His activity in their lives, make the adjustments to Him, and watch God work mightily through them?

———◆———

Imagine having the opportunity, as the apostle John did, of laying your head against the bosom of Christ. What would you learn about the love of God if you could?

Brennan Manning

I believe that you have to pass through the written Word into the living Word and into an intimate heartfelt relationship with Jesus in order to have, as Paul says, "the mind of Christ Jesus." Here's what happens, I think. If, like the apostle John, you lay your head on the breast of Jesus and listen to His heartbeat, you pass beyond intellect and beyond emotion into a higher way of knowing. Heart speaks to heart, or as the provocative French proverb goes, "The heart has her reasons for which the mind knows nothing."

Our God is a loving God. We need others to help encourage us in those times when we doubt the truth of that statement. I asked Max Lucado what convinces him that God is love.

Max Lucado

You can either see God as a loving God or as a judgmental and harsh God. If God is a judgmental and harsh God, we wouldn't be here. We have not met His standards; we have fallen too many times. I think the very fact that I still have breath tells me that God is a loving God, because He has kept me around this long.

If I can accept the fact that God is a loving God, then I can look at the kind of love that He is. His love is not the kind of love we have on earth; it's a divine love. It's a kind of love that doesn't increase if I'm better or decrease if I'm worse. It's a remarkable kind of love that says, "I'm going to love you independent of what you do." You know, my actions have a thermostatic impact on other people's love for me. If I said bad words to you right now, your love for me would diminish. If I said nice words to you, your love might increase. I can impact and control to a certain degree the amount of love people have for me. Not so with God's love. I cannot change His love. I cannot make it more or make it less.

I think that's the most fascinating truth of Scripture and the one thing I wish people understood about God. We frequently have people walk into our building who don't feel loved. I try to tell them, "It's not up to you to decide if you're loved; that's God's decision, and He said, 'I love you with an everlasting love.'"

———

Sometimes the love of God is seen not in any direct action but in the reaction of His people to His calling. Upon hearing the good news of the gospel, shouldn't we who have accepted His forgiveness and grace be changed by the sheer implications of this new reality? Scotty Smith, speaking on the subject of God's love for us, sees that love most readily in the lives of the people around him.

Scotty Smith

It has been a joy to watch the mosaic, the tapestry, that God is putting together in our church—to see men and women not getting more religious but becoming more astonished at how much God loves them and saying, "How then shall I live in light of the revelation of God's grace, mercy, compassion, and will for this creation He has made?"

I think of a couple in our church, Jim and Lynn Henderson. Here's a guy who finished first in his class at Vanderbilt University School of Medicine after having his final year of undergraduate school waived because he was so bright. He finished at the top of his class, got the highest honor given by the medical school, and was offered a partnership in the leading pediatrics group in Nashville.

Jim had been working there for a year when he and his wife found their hearts beating toward the mission field. It wasn't that a missionary had come to the church telling war stories, highlighting all the needs in the world, and saying, "If you don't meet these needs, who will?" Rather, it was a case of an incredibly gifted doctor and his wife moving from legalism, from a life of religious confusion, into a deeper experience of the God of all grace. They began to say, "How then shall we live in light of God's extraordinary love?" Next thing you know, they were exposed to missions, and this past year they moved with their three kids to India. They are investing themselves now among the poorest of the poor, living up in the mountains of India fighting off monkeys. Literally, they've got monkeys—friendly monkeys and not-so-friendly monkeys—where they live!

What a paradox! Anyone in this culture would say, "This guy has a ticket to anything he wants. He can write his salary. He can design his partnership. He can be a pediatrician, retire when he's forty-five, have three extra condos, and take life easy." But here's a man who said, "How boring!" Why do that with your life when, in light of the love of God, you can invest yourself in a way that gives you a part in impacting a whole country with the gospel? My heart gets so thrilled when I watch people get that free. I can take that story and multiply it a hundred times in terms of the men and women I've watched come more fully under the influence of the gospel.

There's a part of me that says, "Lord, it would be so much easier if we were just legalists. If this church were nothing but a bunch of pragmatists, we could create paradigms and programs like so many other churches and be quite successful at it." But growth, revival, and renewal in this church means bringing a greater percentage of the people into a deeper discipleship; then they might be more willing to ask, "Father, what do You want me to do with the rest of my life?"

———◆———

It can be oddly funny when God's kingdom intersects with the way things are supposed to work in our world. Barbara Johnson tells the story of a tragic car accident, a man's miraculous healing, and what it's like explaining to the insurance company that your once-blind husband can see.

Barbara Johnson

My husband, Bill, and I were taking a bunch of young people up to a camp in the mountains. Bill drove on ahead of me and took all the good things—the Cokes, the hot dogs, and the hamburgers. I was behind him by about twenty minutes with two teenagers and two twelve-year-olds in our other car. Driving up the mountain road toward the retreat center, I found a heap of a man in the middle of the road, all covered with blood and glass. It was Bill. The road department had left debris in the road that Bill hadn't seen in the dark, and it caused the accident. I had to leave Bill there on that road and leave all the kids with him while I went about ten miles up the road to get to a telephone to call an ambulance.

The doctors said that Bill would be a vegetable for life, that he would never function as a normal person because he had brain damage. The blood clots in his brain were inoperable, and the prognosis was that he couldn't live more than five years. He had been a lieutenant commander in the navy, so they said, "You can put him in a veterans' hospital, but it will take quite a while to get him in there." So for two years Bill was at home, but he didn't know anybody. He was like a vegetable. He was blind, and my boys helped take care of him.

Just about the time we were going to get him into the veterans' hospital, the Lord touched him and healed him. His sight returned, and he went back to work as an engineer. Insurance had paid us twenty thousand dollars after the accident, so we had to go and explain that Bill was no longer blind and was back at work. But we had already spent the twenty thousand! They said, "Well now, he *was* blind, so you *were* qualified to get the money." Then they said, "We've never had this happen before, so you can keep it."

The Veterans Administration had paid off our house loan. Now can you imagine the VA, after they've paid off a loan, trying to reverse it? It's too much for them to do that, so they just said, "We'll just let it go through." So the house was paid for, we had twenty thousand dollars from the insurance company, and Bill was going back to work!

The last obstacle was the Department of Motor Vehicles. The DMV didn't want to give Bill a driver's license because he had been blind and had brain seizures, and who wanted to give him a road test? It took about a year to convince the DMV that he could drive again. So Bill is quite a miracle. It is a miracle that God brought him through all that.

You know, after the accident we took Bill to Kathryn Kuhlman meetings and other places where people prayed for healing. Nothing happened there. We had lots of prayer, lots of people praying for him. But two years went by, and nothing happened. I thought, *Well then, God's going to do it in His own way in His own time.* And that's how He did it, in His own way and time. It's quite a miracle that he's been able to function all these years. In fact, it has been thirty years since the accident, and he's still here. He says, "I've had thirty years of bonus time, so anytime the Lord takes me now, boy, I'm ready to go."

Barbara has experienced a great deal of tragedy in her life, including the death of two of her children and estrangement from a third. I asked her how a person who has known so much suffering can still have joy.

It's like going through a really dark tunnel. If you know there's a light at the end of the tunnel and it's not another train coming at you, you can go through anything a day at a time. See, God only gives you grace one day at a time. He doesn't give it to you for a month or for the whole trip. Yesterday is a canceled check, tomorrow is a promissory note, but you've got today to live. You need to get up in the morning and say, "This is my day to serve the Lord. I've got one day, twenty-four hours, to serve Him." You can do anything one day at a time.

I've learned to say, "Whatever, Lord," which has been like a magic phrase for me. No matter what comes into my life, "though He slay me," as Job said, "yet will I trust in Him." It's a prayer of relinquishment: "Whatever, Lord. Whatever comes through Your filter, I know Your grace will get me through it." This prayer has worked for me, and it has worked for the many parents I've talked to who are trying to work through the loss of a child. We work with many parents who've lost a child through death, many parents who have children in jail. Last year we had 350 families who lost a child through AIDS.

How do I keep from being completely depressed after absorbing all this pain? After I speak with each one of these parents, I pray with them; I pray that God's comfort blanket will surround them. Afterward I pray, "Now Lord, help me to windshield-wipe that problem. I will continue to pray for that person, but I need You to windshield-wipe the past so I can go on to the next person." You can't carry yesterday's load today. That old baggage has got to go. New baggage is coming up, and you can carry just so much at a time.

Beyond that, I think God does have to give you a gift of joy. Joy is like God living in the marrow of your bones. It's a gift that God has given me. I don't have a lot of faith. I readily admit that. I don't have a lot of a lot of things, but I do have a lot of joy. When I travel with the Women of Faith conferences, I always say, "I don't know why I'm with this group. I don't have a lot of faith, but I've got joy." And that's all I really need.

———

"Jesus didn't die to make me nice, He died to make me His," *says Steve Brown, explaining the danger of trying to earn God's* *love and forgiveness.*

Steve Brown

This is what the gospel is: God is not mad at His people; and if other people will go to Him, He will not be mad at them either because of the cross. We hate that. We want to pay, so off to work we go; it's really important that we not owe. The sign of man's fall is this tendency to be drawn into an "I can earn it" mentality. We have to fight that all the time.

If we allow God's Spirit to speak to us, the most dangerous thing we can say is, "Lord show me myself"—because He will do it. I think fallen nature is manifested for the Christian not so much in terms of the sins we commit but in terms of the purity we commit. The danger is that we can become pharisaical. You've never met a man who wants to be obedient more than I do, and I'm better at it than I used to be. But Jesus didn't die to make me nice; He died to make me His. And out of that flows any obedience that I have.

———

Sometimes our moods and mind-sets can get in the way of appreciating God's love. He surprises us with that love when we choose to establish an attitude of gratitude.

Patsy Clairmont

I'm a whiny traveler. I don't think I'm a gracious woman when it comes to packing and unpacking suitcases. I've never learned how to do that well; it doesn't come naturally. I don't like dragging through airports. I get bored on long flights—and a long flight to me is anything over an hour. It was never my desire to travel. My natural tendency was to be agoraphobic, which left me housebound for a time. My house and the immediate surroundings are still my greatest comfort zone. I believe it was through God's grace and mercy that I was called into a ministry that continually dragged me away from my comfort zone. I found out that He is my comfort zone; anywhere I go, He goes.

As long as I want to whine and cry when I travel, He gives me the freedom to do that. The Israelites did it for forty years, and if I want to do it for forty more years, I can. But I'm the one who pays the price. The other option is that I could enter into this journey with a grateful heart. That was one of the things that was very helpful about traveling and ministering with Florence Littauer. When I would meet up with her at an airport or a hotel, she would always say, "Aren't we fortunate that we are allowed to do something that we love to do?"

And she was right. I love doing what I do once I get where I am going. It's the traveling back and forth that is the drag. I have to ask God continually to help me adjust my attitude about the travel experience. I notice that when my attitude is better about it, it is less draining for me; and I am open to some very special surprises that God often brings along the way.

How do we know God is real? Some of us seem to have been born with a faith that never really doubts. The reality of God just makes more sense than any alternative. But for others, doubts sprout up like weeds in a flower bed. I asked Patsy to do a little gardening.

I know God is real because of what He has done in my own interior being. I got to such a place of desperation in my life that I decided I was through with trying all my own ways and knowing all my own answers. I was willing to say, "If You are there and if You care, then do something to rescue me; and I will obey You to the best of my ability." When I got to that place, I began to experience God in many different ways. I could see His handiwork. The Bible says that the heavens declare His glory, and I could see glorious things about God. I could see His fingerprints all over creation. What I needed was to experience those fingerprints inside my own heart.

My husband had to have open-heart surgery because he had blockages behind his heart. The doctors had to saw through his breastbone, pull open the rib cage to expose the chest cavity, reach in, and lift out his heart. They told me, "At one point your husband's heart will be in the hand of a surgeon." And I remember saying, "Oh, he's going to get fingerprints all over it."

That reminds me of our God—how He loves to examine the heart. He's not satisfied with just seeing a mind or an attitude; He wants to look at the very deepest part of the heart. It's as if He lifts it out and examines it. That was what I needed done to me many years ago, and that is what I experienced. It was not easy. There was a breaking, so to speak, as He sawed through and exposed the deepest secrets of my life.

A speaker named Ney Bailey said something once that was so wonderful. It was a question she posed that's used now at the Women of Faith conferences: If there was a video made of your entire life—including everything you've ever thought, everything you've said that you thought no one would ever know about—and it was shown at a local theater to all your family and friends, how would you feel? That's a devastating and frightening thought! Then Ney said, "God has seen your movie, and He loves you." That is what I experienced as He exposed the most frightening parts of my life to the light. I found that I was safe in that examination. He already knew everything there was to know about me—and He still cared passionately for me!

What's the Secret?

Since perfect love can't give us second best, we know that everything that comes into our lives has been filtered through God's love with our best interests in mind. God's love for us is so great, it can't be contained in a simple chapter of a book. This chapter may be finite, but His love goes on and on and on.

Secret #6

In our lives, dark days come and dark days go, just like storms on the Weather Channel. But God never changes. When we're in the middle of a storm, we can rely on other Christians who love us, and the Word of God to get through. In our lives, dark days come and dark days go, just

Into Every Life
a Little Rain Will Pour

The Weather Channel is on, and a meteorologist is standing in front of one of those gigantic, electronic satellite maps. The forty-eight contiguous states are shaded green and separated by thin black lines. Flashing at different points are descriptive lay-terms for weather—like "HOT" or "SHOWERS" or "CHILLY"—spelled out in lettering that looks just like those words feel. A quick glance shows that some states have skies that are as clear as a bell, while others have dark, ominous storm clouds warning of imminent adverse weather. How strange it is that San Diego, California, will enjoy a sunny, eighty-five degree day, and people there will head to the beach; while in St. Louis, Missouri, a tornado watch is on, and people there will be heading for shelter. Tomorrow's prediction? All new weather, of course! Hot, cold, sunny, rainy—everything switches places.

In life, just as on the Weather Channel, storms pop up unexpectedly. Dark clouds appear on the horizon and worry us. Gusts of wind rustle about, unsettling our relationships and our lives. Sometimes wild tornadoes or gigantic tropical storms blow in seemingly from nowhere and ravage everything around us. Why? What's going on here? We're Christians, after all. Shouldn't life be a little less messy?

Well, actually…

Like the old adage goes, into every life a little rain will pour. Or as Jesus put it in John 16:33, "In this world you will have trouble." Many excellent books have been written about the trouble that Jesus spoke of. They address the "why" question and provide knowing answers: God is testing us; God is molding us; we're sinful people living in a sinful world—what else can you expect? These books are popular because we want to understand adversity. We think that if we understand it, we can survive it and perhaps even avoid it in the future.

But adversity is something we can't control, as much as we would like to. It's a part of life, and life can't be controlled. There is, however, something we can control when it comes to trouble, and that's our response. How we respond to difficulty is something we can control—but only if we rely on Christ. Many problems are bigger than you or me, but none is greater than the Lord.

The authors in this chapter speak candidly about the crises they have bravely faced and sometimes barely survived. They believe they're better people for having gone through these struggles. But surviving life's darkest nights, its sharpest arrows, and its coldest winters requires much more than mere bravery. As Chris Matthews, host of the MSNBC program *Hardball*, once put it: "It's an awfully big ocean out there, and we're in an awfully small boat."

The authors in this chapter have learned to rely on much more than their own small boats, and so should you and I. They rely on faith, prayer, family and friends, the Bible, and God's Holy Spirit. They stay closest to Christ when the night is darkest. They remember His promises, His power, and who they are in Him. The challenges they've collectively faced haven't been easy. They've dealt with such issues as depression, chronic illness, estrangement, confusion, and anxiety disorders. They've battled alcohol abuse, criticism, burnout, and brokenness. They've endured the loss of career and the loss of loved ones; but thankfully, it's the loss of their reliance on anything but the power of Christ that's pulled each one through. And He will pull you through as well.

We want to believe we can arrive at a place in life where we'll be protected from further pain and sorrow. In this chapter, however, our bright, successful, popular, and acclaimed authors contradict the myth that any such place exists on earth. Let me make it clear by saying it another way: Becoming wealthy, famous, or powerful doesn't immunize anyone from illnesses, difficulties, sorrows, or conflicts. We can't escape problems in life, no matter what our status or resources.

You and I can learn something important from the authors' stories about their own times of difficulty and challenge. We can learn to move closer to the heart of God, just as they did. He is the only source for our security in this troubled world.

What should we do during the inevitable dark times? The secret to surviving the rainy days in life is knowing that they *will* come— and when they do, remaining confident that God is in control. In John 16:33 Jesus said, "In this world you will have trouble." But then He added these wonderful words: "But take heart! I have overcome the world."

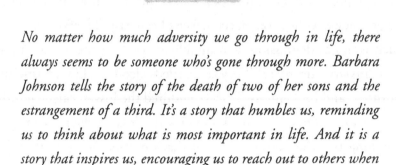

No matter how much adversity we go through in life, there always seems to be someone who's gone through more. Barbara Johnson tells the story of the death of two of her sons and the estrangement of a third. It's a story that humbles us, reminding us to think about what is most important in life. And it is a story that inspires us, encouraging us to reach out to others when they need to be scraped off the ceiling.

Barbara Johnson

I had four sons. The first one was a beautiful Christian boy named Steve who wanted to go into the marines. He wasn't quite eighteen, and I didn't want him to go. But a lot of his friends were going in, and he really wanted to go too. So three months before his eighteenth birthday I went down to the recruiting office and signed the papers so he could join. By the time he had his eighteenth birthday he didn't want to be in the marines anymore, but it was too late! Once you sign, you are in.

He had hardly finished his training when he was sent to Vietnam. We knew he was a Christian and loved the Lord, so when we got the word that he had been killed, it was a relief in a way. Every day we read in the newspaper about losing thousands and thousands of boys in Vietnam. When it finally happened it was almost like, "Well, he's safe in the arms of Jesus." We sang a song with those words in church the day he left to go into the service, and then we sang it again at his memorial service.

another deposit

Exactly five years from the day I buried that boy, our twenty-three-year-old son, Tim, was killed on his way home from a trip to Alaska. He and his friend had gone up there for the summer between college semesters. While he was there, he was baptized. It kind of hurt my feelings to read about his baptism in his letter because he had already been baptized at our home church, and I figured we had good water too.

Anyway, he called me on the first of August to say he was on his way home. He told me the Lord had really touched his heart. He said, "I've got a sparkle in my eye and a spring in my step, and I'll be home in five days to tell you what the Lord has done." Understand, he was a Christian boy when he went up there. He came from a Christian family and a Christian school. But something happened that touched his heart in a special way when he was in Alaska.

That night, my husband, my two sons, and I were sitting around the dinner table, marveling over Tim's change. "What's happened to this kid?" we wondered. We were very excited about seeing him. That's when we got a call from the Royal Canadian Mounted Police telling us that some drunken boys in a truck had hit Tim's little car, and Tim had been ushered immediately into the presence of God.

I thought, *This is not fair. I just talked to him!* His voice was still ringing in my ears. He was going to be home in five days. How could this be? I was mad at God. I remember running through the house crying, "This isn't fair! I've got one deposited in heaven, and I don't need another!"

In God's economy over time, I could see that God used that accident as a blessing. He took Tim at a time when he was closest to the Lord, and many young people came to the Lord through his story. Campus Life and Youth for Christ put his story in their magazines. "Their Death Was Only the Beginning" was the name of the article.

scraped off the ceiling

So we started out with four boys, and now two were in heaven. We have a third son named Barney. He is married and has a nice family. He's OK. We learned that the fourth one, Larry, was homosexual the year after Tim was killed. I didn't know how to handle that revelation because I didn't know anyone who was homosexual, and Christians didn't talk about it. There was nobody to talk to. Silence and loneliness were the hardest things to deal with. My husband went off to work and said, "It's just a phase." At home I quoted Bible verses at Larry about abomination, going to hell—you know the kind. I said a lot of unloving and uncaring things. Because of that, he disappeared for eleven years. He went into the lifestyle, disowned us, changed his name, and said he never wanted to see us again.

I spent eleven years in God's waiting room. I promised God if He would get me through this crisis and I didn't end up in a home for the bewildered, I would start a support group for Christian parents who experience the same kind of loss. I thought I was going to die; and when you think you are going to die, you promise God anything. I never would have made that promise if I had thought I was going to live!

We started a group called Spatula Ministries for parents. When parents have this kind of trouble with their children, they land on the ceiling, and we scrape them off with the spatula of love. We've been meeting for twenty years now at Crystal Cathedral in Garden

Grove, California. Thousands of parents have come through Spatula Ministries from all over the country and all over the world. It helps when they have somebody they can talk to and let out their pain. See, openness is to holiness what secrets are to sickness. If you don't let pain out and talk about it, you get sick—and we want parents to get well.

Suffering, the Bible says, serves a purpose in our lives. I asked Barbara what she thinks that purpose is.

The iron crown of suffering precedes the golden crown of glory. When you're going through suffering—that fiery furnace time—you need to realize that God is using that time to prepare you. He's using that time to pare you down, to fine-tune you, so you can become a better counselor, a better Christian, more devoted to your family. Suffering produces that in us. It produces a big chunk of gold in our lives. The people I know who have never suffered, never gone through a loss, never gone through anything, don't have the same depth as those who've lost a child or been through some other pain.

Young people are not longing for heaven. I know I wasn't when I was twenty and thirty. But after living through what I've lived through, and the older I get, the more wonderful heaven seems to me.

I used to say, "Why me? Why did I lose two kids? Why did my husband have an accident? Why did my son disappear for eleven years?" But then I learned to say the prayer of relinquishment: "Whatever, Lord." Job said, "Although He slay me, yet will I trust in Him." When I say, "Whatever, Lord," I mean, "Whatever You send into my life, I trust that Your filter is large enough to accommodate it." Since learning to say that prayer I've had this beautiful bubble of joy that's based on trust and faith in God. I have been able to look at everything that has happened in my life and everything that's happening now and say, "Whatever, Lord." I think that's the secret. I would encourage people to get off the "Why me?" kick and start saying, "Whatever, Lord." God's grace is sufficient for all of us.

———————

Another kind of difficulty many people face is the frustration of trying to get somewhere professionally, even relationally, and yet each day seems to bring more struggle than reprieve. This story from Frank Peretti reminds us to never give up, even when things seem hopeless.

Frank Peretti

I have very seldom felt like quitting. I've identified with a lot of characters who've had to struggle but who never gave up. I still remember the old *Rocky* movies with Sylvester Stallone as a boxer, trying to stay on his feet for fifteen rounds against the champ, Apollo Creed. I really identified with that film when it first came out because that was my life at the time. It felt like I was getting beaten to death, and I wasn't getting anywhere. Nothing was connecting. I wanted to be a writer, but I couldn't get a publisher. I was working in a factory. I had been in the ministry and had burned out of that, so I felt like a failure.

But quitting was never an option for me. I figured, "Well, I'm going to go down in flames, or I'm going to drop dead, but I'm not going to give up!" I just kept going. I remember seeing pictures of some of the Olympic marathon runners limping across the finish line on their last leg. Those images are so vivid. I identified with them too. I said, "That's me. I'm going to drop dead before I give up. I'm going to make it across that finish line one way or another." I think the Lord was working in my life to teach me the importance of being steadfast and hanging in there.

My first book, *This Present Darkness,* took about a year and a half to finally take off. I remember being very hopeful that it would do well. I was working in a ski factory at the time, and I remember going to the telephone every month during one of my lunch or coffee breaks and calling the publisher to find out how many books had sold the previous month. Then I'd do the arithmetic, trying to figure out how much money I might make and whether I'd ever make enough to get out of the factory. I never heard much good news during those calls.

Back at the factory we had an expression: "going over the wall." It was as if the factory were a prison, and if somebody found some other line of work or something else to do, they'd escaped! "Did you hear about so and so? He went over the wall!" I identified with the Count of Monte Cristo. Here's a guy unjustly accused of a crime and thrown into a French prison. He decides he's got to escape, so he starts chiseling his way out. I mean, it takes him years to chisel his way through those solid rock walls, using only a piece of metal and a crude hammer he made from a rock. That's the way I felt at the factory. I was going to get out of there one way or another!

Even as the book seemed to languish, I was getting ready to do the next project. I thought, *OK, what else can I do?* I was thinking about getting into radio drama or television. In fact, I was still working at the factory when James Dobson's Focus on the Family did a broadcast of my book *Tilly*, and I heard it on my radio there on my workbench at the factory. At that point I was working on the sequel to *This Present Darkness* called *Piercing the Darkness*. I was determined! I really felt the Lord had called me to be a writer, and since I didn't have anything else that I knew I wanted to do, that's what I pursued.

There was a weird period of waiting there; things were a little iffy. But one day, a year and a half after *This Present Darkness* came out, I called the publisher, and he sounded really happy. He said, "We sold four thousand copies last month!" That was a big deal! But then the next month we sold about twenty thousand, and then about forty thousand, and then sixty thousand, and then we started seeing some incredible numbers. It just came out of a slingshot, and it was really pretty miraculous. Not long after, of course, I got an advance from the publisher that was big enough to allow me to leave the factory and write full-time, and I've been a full-time writer ever since. I went over the wall! I remember that moment, you better believe it. Oh, what a moment!

At age thirty-six Sheila Walsh walked away from her role as co-host of the 700 Club *with Pat Robertson and admitted herself to a psychiatric hospital to treat her depression. Although it felt like the end to Sheila, she discovered it was actually a new beginning.*

Sheila Walsh

I read a quote by Eleanor Roosevelt in which she said, "You must do the things you are afraid of, because it's only in facing your fears that you will ever be free." I've found that to be absolutely true in my own life. If you had asked me as a teenager what was my greatest fear, I would have said, "That I would end up like my dad." He ended up in a psychiatric hospital when he was thirty-four. Well, I ended up in a psychiatric hospital when I was thirty-five or thirty-six. It is one of the greatest things to face your greatest fears. When you walk through them, stumbling at times, you come out with bloody knees; but you come out on the other side with a greater understanding not only of the grace and love of God, but of the fact that He can take you through anything.

After I got out of the psychiatric hospital, I met with a counselor—a very godly man—three times a week for three years. It was a discipleship relationship more than anything else. One of the most profound things he said to me was, "Sheila, Jesus has not come to get you through this; He's come to live in you through this." That's why, when I stand up in front of fifteen thousand women on any given weekend, I need to know that what I say from that platform is true: God will sustain you, whether you've just been diagnosed with breast cancer or your husband just left you for another woman or your child did not come home from the hospital. I understand Romans chapter five more than I ever did before: "We also rejoice in our sufferings, because we know that suffering produces perseverance; perseverance, character; and character, hope; and hope does not disappoint us."

I asked Sheila, "Did you ever feel hopeless?"

When you go through something that's your worst personal nightmare, when you pray at night that you won't wake up in the morning—I've felt that. I never considered taking my life, but there were times I did not want to wake up in the morning. I remember praying, "God, if there is any mercy left in Your heart for me, please take me home." Since I went through my hospitalization I've had dark moments, but I've never felt hopeless.

We have this bizarre idea that if you love God enough and live a fairly decent life, life will be easy. There's nothing in Scripture to support that. Christ said, "In this world you will have tribulations. But don't worry, because I've overcome what is in this world." I still have dark days; in fact, yesterday was one of them. I felt sad all day for no particular reason. So I went out to my car, put on some music, and I began to sing to the Lord.

That's what I love about the psalms of David. They were not supposed to be something we read for five minutes at night, then we close the book and go to bed. Those were the songs of the church that the people sang together, and they sang them out loud. They sang out their pain and they sang out their joy, and that's what I do too. That's what I encourage people to do who struggle as I have with depression. Get out your Bible, open to Psalms, and pray them aloud. Pray them on days when tears are rolling down your face, and pray them on the days when you are laughing.

———

For years Patsy Clairmont suffered with the anxiety disorder agoraphobia—the fear of open spaces. When you consider all that Patsy has accomplished in her career, it's remarkable to think how restrictive this disorder once was for her. She discusses what it was like living with agoraphobia and how she found freedom from being housebound.

Patsy Clairmont

The difference between agoraphobia and, let's say, arachnophobia—the fear of spiders—is that with arachnophobia you have one fear. It may be intense, it may be huge, it may dominate your life, but it's one fear. When you are an agoraphobic, however, you have collected many fears. You are a cluster of fears. If you look up *agoraphobia* in the dictionary, you read that it's the fear of open places, open spaces. But the way it manifests itself in your life is that you allow many different things to become intimidating.

When people exhibit an extreme emotion, that emotion is usually their hiding place from the thing they're most afraid of. For instance, people who are extremely full of fear are usually very, very angry people. But it is too scary for them to touch all that volatile anger, so they end up refuging in their fear. That's their hiding place. They feel safer and more in control in their fear than in their bigger, deeper issue of anger. As for me, I refuged in fear. I was afraid of everything. I wasn't purposing to hide from my anger and not resolve it; I wasn't aware that that's what I was doing.

My fears were unreasonable. They didn't make sense. For instance, I was afraid of getting in an elevator, but I would put my children in one. I knew beyond a doubt they would be safe, but it was not safe for me. That's not reasonable. Why would it be safe for them and not me? I had a tremendous fear of storms, heights, and doctors, and yet I was calling my doctor for help all the time. My fears just didn't make sense because they were not authentic fear. They were the acting out, the refuge place. The deeper issue was that I had a lot of anger that came out of woundedness and hurt, and that needed to be addressed before the Lord.

How did I get well? One baby step at a time. I would love to tell people that I just went to bed one night and rose up righteous the next morning. I would love to make it easier for them. But the truth is I had to pick up one foot and place it in front of the other when I did not feel like doing it. I had to start with the littlest details of life.

I remember crying out to the Lord, saying I wanted to do great things for Him. And I remember the unfolding of a thought inside of me from the Lord: "Go make your bed." I couldn't figure that out. I thought, *What does making my bed have to do with doing great things for God?* And it kept unfolding inside of me, "Go make your bed, go make your bed." I remember standing in front of that bed, looking at it, and saying to the Lord, "Do I have to make both sides? I only slept on this side. Shouldn't you-know-who have to make his own side?" And He said, "No, I want you to make both sides, and I want you to do it every day." That didn't make sense to me, but I determined that I was going to obey Him. Not that I was initially so compliant; I was an exceedingly rebellious young woman! But by that time I was so broken and desperate that I was willing to do whatever He asked.

So I began making the bed every day. And after a week, thinking I'd been a great success, I said, "Now can I go do something big for You?"

"Yes," He said. "Go wash the dishes."

Well, I thought, *how dull and boring!* But I found a principle in the Scripture that says when you are faithful in the little things, then He will entrust you with more. That was my journey out of agoraphobia—learning to be faithful in little things before the Lord.

No one is exempt from struggle in life, as Max Lucado attests. While difficulties may come in different forms to different people, we all have struggle in common.

Max Lucado

Just last night we began our prayer service at the church with my own confession of struggles that I have. I don't think the church is interested in seeing how perfect I am. They need to know that I have burdens too. Though I have been away from alcohol for more than twenty years, I think I can say there's not a week that goes by that I don't think, *Boy, a drink would be good.* It's not a hounding temptation to me, but the devil's there; and if I'm not prayerful and careful, I could fall again.

There has never been a time when I've felt as if I have arrived. For one, there is always the challenge of pride when I hear people say, "You've got a message to share; you're anointed"—things like that. Charles Spurgeon once said that you need to keep just enough encouragement to stay encouraged, but then give the rest of it back. That's what I try to do. God spoke through a donkey. He came to Jerusalem on the back of a mule. So if I help bring Jesus into a place, it's not because I'm the one who's so good. I have to keep that attitude, and it's not always easy.

———

Ministers are particularly prone to burnout in their work. Scotty Smith, who was on an extended sabbatical during our interview, spoke openly about the danger of depleting yourself physically and spiritually while trying to care for the needs of others.

Scotty Smith

One of the things we realized in our church is that if we take seriously the preaching of God's grace, then broken and hurting people will come out of the woodwork. That's one of the reasons this church is growing so fast. We have a "sinner safe" church. That doesn't mean we're promoting sin; but it's assumed that if you're a human being, you're falling short of the glory of God. As our numbers have grown, we've seen more opportunity to access broken marriages, broken minds, and broken beings. And as weakness, neediness, hurt, and sin has multiplied, so have the taxing effects on the leadership.

How does a leadership family really love the large numbers of people it's inviting to be honest about their struggles? What we've realized, and what led me to take this sabbatical, is this: If you're not wise and careful, you can expend so much energy trying to care for people that your own resources get depleted. You suddenly find yourself physically, emotionally, and spiritually bankrupt. It took three weeks into this sabbatical for me to realize how close to total burnout I was.

If you are involved in a legalistic church, you can reduce everything to formulas. You can reduce everything to nice little packaged teachings. If someone comes into your office and says, "My marriage is hurting," you can say, "Go to this family life conference, read this book, do this, do that, obey, take three in the morning, and call me next month." If your paradigm of spirituality is simply rules and obedience, things don't get that messy. But if you know the gospel, you realize that the Father is not simply rearranging deck furniture on the *Titanic*. He's changing our hearts. And that makes you get far more involved in people's hearts and lives.

There have been times when I've felt like quitting. There have been times when I've felt like I used to feel back when I told God I'll never be a pastor. I've thought, *Lord, I'm overwhelmed. It's too much!* But truly, the longer I am alive and the more I understand the gospel, the more short-lived those seasons are. It has been said that the church is like Noah's ark; if it weren't for the storm outside, you couldn't stand the stink inside! Life in the body of Christ is very messy, and until we're glorified there is going to be pettiness, failure, and people bailing. There's going to be longings, confusion, fear, and pain.

At times I think I'd really rather do something else. Maybe Ed McMahon will show up, or I'll win the lottery. I'll move to Montana, fly-fish, and write books. Those moments are profound, they are powerful, and they are real. But the gospel brings me back to my sanity and I say, "Lord, I'm not my own. You call me to live wisely. You call me to pace myself. You know what You're doing, and I trust You."

During his lifetime, Brennan Manning has been a minister to the poor, a marine, a Franciscan priest, a theology instructor, a campus minister, and perhaps most surprisingly, an alcoholic. Why does a person become an alcoholic? Brennan explained.

Brennan Manning

I don't know anyone who ever chose to be an alcoholic. Nobody says, "When I grow up, I want to be an alcoholic. What a great way to live!" The people I know who are alcoholics, including myself, have had some kind of genetic predisposition to alcoholism. That means we can't drink alcohol like a normal person can. After the first taste of alcohol, it becomes like a narcotic in the system. It creates a craving. As the old saw goes, "The drunk takes a drink, then the drink takes a drink, then the drink takes the drunk." That phenomenon of craving, that physical inability to stop, is at the essence of alcoholism. That's why it's called a biopsychological disease by the American Medical Association.

My family has a history of alcoholism. Back in Brooklyn, New York, I really didn't know anybody who didn't drink alcohol. The gene plus the environment that I was raised in contributed to my being an alcoholic—the predisposition plus the availability.

The first thing that I did to recover was to go to a place called Hazelden in Minnesota. It's the granddaddy of all the alcohol and drug rehab centers in the United States. I had several months of treatment there. First I went through a medically supervised detoxification and withdrawal from alcohol, because it can be extremely dangerous to stop cold turkey. Then I had an intense introduction to alcoholism, looking at the physical, mental, emotional, and spiritual sides of the disease.

But my time at Hazelden was just the beginning. The alcoholics who are sober day in and day out, year in and year out, are the ones who attend Alcoholics Anonymous meetings. They diligently work through the twelve steps of recovery, talk regularly with their sponsor, and read the Big Book, which is like the inspired book for the alcoholic community. Eighty-five percent of people who stay sober today do so through the Alcoholics Anonymous program.

———◆———

Through all our stumbling in life, God is there. Through our weaknesses, our shortcomings, our confusion, and our foolish-

ness, He is ever-present, gently revealing Himself to us. He uses a lifetime of experiences to convince us that we need Him.

Larry Crabb

If I ever were to write an autobiography, I think I'd call it *Sovereign Stumbling.* I stumble, and God is sovereign. In college I chose to major in psychology because I didn't like anything else. There was no deep sense of "I want to be a psychologist to be useful to the Lord." I wanted to make a living. I didn't like chemistry, so that ruled out medicine; and I'm lousy at math, so that ruled out engineering. All that was left, I thought, was psychology. My choices in those days were incredibly immature, but looking back I can see the hand of God. He was saying, "I'm going to make you into a troubled, tortured mess so you'll be more aware of how badly you long to connect with others, and maybe you'll be able to speak about it someday."

bigger than life

Our celebrity culture is awful. It's just awful. I was speaking to ten thousand people three weeks ago, and a week later I was speaking to two thousand people. As I sat there in the audience waiting to be introduced to this huge crowd, I found myself thinking, *I've got to get up and do my shtick. I've got to do my thing. Nobody here knows me, but I can tell a funny story. I can teach the Bible, I can make points, and people are going to applaud; people are going to say I'm good.* I almost wanted to scream and run out of the place shouting obscenities at the top of my lungs. I thought, *This is a ridiculous culture in which we live. People are assuming that I'm something that's not anything close to what I really am.*

In Henri Nouwen's last book, *Sabbatical Journey*, he made the comment that anybody who's worth anything preaches a message far bigger than his or her life. I believe I'm preaching a message that's so much bigger than my life. I don't know how to relate to my kids half the time. They're both grown; they're twenty-eight and thirty-one years of age at the time of this writing, and they've gone through their share of struggles. There are times I haven't got a clue what to do. My wife and I attended a very difficult family funeral a week ago, and in the middle of that, I let her down. When she let me know that I'd disappointed her, I got furious! I don't know how to connect. I know I want to connect, and there have been times when the Lord has provided for me. But my gosh, in the core of my soul, I'm a mess!

My wife and I are part of a group of four couples in which at least one partner in each couple is an author. We've been together for five years now. The reason we formed this little group was to have a place where we could get off the stage and be real. That's a terrible commentary, I think. It took us two years before each of us admitted that we were intimidated by the others. That's crazy!

just a fellow struggler

So if anybody wants to listen to what I have to say, they should do a couple things. One, measure what I say against the Scripture. Don't follow me, for goodness sake. But if I'm saying something that resonates within your spiritual heart and seems to be consistent with the Scripture, follow it, because you want to follow God, not me. And two, remember that I'm a fellow struggler. I know that can sound like a nice preacher comment, but I'm just journeying along with everybody else. There are times I'm depressed, times I get mad, times a bad word comes out of my mouth. There are times I do things that are totally not what the Lord would have me do. I'm just learning about brokenness and I'm learning the meaning of the word grace. It's by grace that God is putting up with me, that He actually likes me and He wants to use me. To me, that's a miracle.

In the phrase of Saint John of the Cross, I've lived in the "dark night of the soul." I'm known by the people who know me well as someone who lives in more dark than sunny days. Oh, there are days that I just struggle. I said to my wife two weeks ago, "I want to cancel the next six months and forget about people."

Recently I've been saying to my wife and a few others, "I wonder, what does it mean to really love Jesus?" It occurred to me about two weeks ago that I love the people I know best—my wife, my kids, a few friends—more than I love Christ, because I know them better. I've been saved for forty-some years, and I still don't love Christ like I want to. Let me just give up and play golf!

I have days like that a lot, but when you face your life honestly, you find out that there's something indestructible in your soul that's a miracle of grace. The Holy Spirit and the new nature are really within me, even when I'm at my very worst. When you embrace your worst, and you're with somebody else in the presence of your worst, then I think you discover the gold that God has put in the core of each of us.

Throughout the centuries the Bible has given readers inspirational and encouraging stories about the heroes of the faith and the faithfulness of God. Henry Blackaby shares how the Word of God has steadied his life even in the midst of trouble.

Henry Blackaby

We've been through some tough, tough times in our family. My wife almost died, and my daughter had cancer. I had a son who decided not to walk closely with the Lord. We've had times when finances were scarce. I've been in the middle of things that were way beyond me. But I've never found myself discouraged in the sense that most people use the term. I've always felt it would be very difficult to stand in the presence of a Holy God who is everything He says He is, look into His face, know what He's like, and be discouraged.

All the way through the Bible, the people God chose were put in situations that were way beyond themselves—for instance, Moses with Pharaoh. But Moses knew that once he heard from God, it didn't matter what Pharaoh said or how Pharaoh threatened. Pharaoh could not cancel what God had said. I look at Abraham, who went out with just a handful of men and a few allies to defeat the kings who had just defeated five other kings. But Abraham knew God would bring the victory, so he didn't get discouraged. When Daniel was thrown into the lion's den, he didn't get discouraged because he knew God.

One biblical hero who was broken over what he knew from God was Jeremiah. His heart cried out because he knew that God was about to destroy His own people. He knew that if they didn't turn back to God, judgment would come, and it would be very thorough. That broke Jeremiah's heart. I don't think he was discouraged in the sense that he thought the situation was hopeless. He did want to get out of the assignment, but he couldn't, he said, because God's Word burned in him. He couldn't not do the will of God.

I've been in many, many situations in which I've faced opposition. I didn't know what was coming next. I didn't know the future of some things. But it never crossed my mind to leave the ministry. I always thought of those moments as my greatest opportunities to experience God. I always said, "Lord, put me in the most difficult, impossible situation, because whatever happens next, it will have to be You. I want to know You, and if I can handle it on my own, I probably won't be calling on You. But if I can't handle it, You're going to have to intervene, and then I'll come to a great experience with You."

I stay in the Scriptures and the Spirit of God, knowing that I'm going to encounter those tough times. God has already put in place the truths about Himself that are going to be important for me to know and to adjust to when those times come. When I hit those discouraging moments, I know that God has already got everything in place that I need to face those moments. Though I've never faced them before, they're not a surprise to God. If I can keep my faith and trust in Him and not look at circumstances, then I can go through any situation.

———

Those whom God uses often go through a time of breaking. I asked Steve Brown to talk about his own "dark night of the soul."

Steve Brown

Generally, if God is going to use someone, whether they are gifted naturally or not, they go through a breaking experience. Saint John of the Cross calls it the "dark night of the soul." Sometimes that breaking is physical, sometimes it's financial, sometimes it's moral. God brings them to the end of themselves so they recognize that there is no solution except God.

Almost everybody I know in ministry has gone through that period. Go back to Harry Emerson Fosdick in the early twentieth century. He was a great preacher, and he had a major nervous breakdown when he was in his thirties. I went through a period in my own life when I left the pastorate, when the wheels came off my wagon. Nobody knew it because I faked it better than Fosdick. I was traveling 150 days a year, putting out a book a year, doing five broadcasts a week, and trying to be a father and a pastor. One night around midnight, after being up since four in the morning, I was sitting in the study crying, and I didn't know why. I said, "God, I didn't ask for any of this stuff. You gave it to me. I didn't plan it, I didn't search for it; You gave it to me. And I didn't love these people when I came here. You made me love them. I've got to do all this stuff until I die, and I'd rather die."

Now I'm not a contemplative or mystic or anything like that. But in that study that night there was such an overwhelming sense of the presence of God. Have you ever opened your Bible and put your finger on a verse? That night I flipped open the Bible, and my eyes fell on the verse, "You shall go out with joy." And at that moment I felt such a release.

But it was a very difficult breaking time for me. It was just horrible. You know that old sermon illustration about the wayward lamb? The shepherd will break the lamb's leg and carry it on his shoulders until the leg heals, and then the lamb will never go away from the shepherd. I think God allows things to come into our lives that let us know how terribly sinful and weak we are. God told the apostle Paul, "My power is made perfect in weakness." I don't think we believe that. We think power is made perfect in might, in money, and in fame—but it's not. His power is made perfect in weakness.

———

When life seems the most difficult—and even when life seems great—it's important to remember who we are in Christ.

Chonda Pierce

This year I've had some really sweet success in earthly terms, and I praise the Lord for that. But what I've learned the most this year is who I am in Christ. All the successes pale in comparison to really understanding that I am a daughter of the King of kings. That's better than a gold record on the wall. If you really, really grasp who you are in Christ, you can't help but be amazed.

What's the Secret?

In our lives, dark days come and dark days go, just like the storms on the Weather Channel. But God never changes. When we're in the middle of the hard times, we can rely on Christ, other Christians who love us, and the Word of God to get us through.

Secret #7

Prayer Is like Bread— We Can Go without It Just So Long

I can still remember waking up early one morning in downtown Chicago. It was the middle of winter, and I was in town on business, staying just a few blocks off Michigan Avenue. From the fourteenth floor of my hotel, the view of the Chicago skyline in the foreground and Lake Michigan in the background was spectacular. But my mind was not on the view; it was on the bagel shop fourteen stories down and half a block away. I'd seen it when I'd arrived the night before, and I couldn't wait to get down there and buy breakfast. Besides, someone with what I can only describe as Einstein-like brilliance had gone into business selling coffee right next-door. Genius!

In a flash I threw on my coat and hit the elevator. Outside, the air blowing off the lake was bitterly cold, and it stung my face as I hurried down the street. I knew it had been worth braving the sub-zero temperatures, however, as soon as I pushed open the bagel shop door. Oven-warmed air came blasting out, and fast on its heels was the rich, satisfying aroma of freshly baked croissants, muffins, and—ah, yes!—bagels. I would have walked nine frozen city blocks for just one whiff of the scent that filled my nostrils at that moment!

Inside, large metal bakery baskets filled with onion, garlic, cinnamon, raisin, wheat, plain, and yeast bagels hung on orange brick walls behind the counter. On my left stood a large wall cooler stocked with plain and flavored whipped cream cheeses. On my right, a doorway led to the coffee shop that was at that moment delivering the fresh-brewed smell of the java I craved. It was perfect—one of those rare scenes in which no one even thought to complain about standing in line. Within minutes I was headed back up to the fourteenth floor to enjoy the view, eat those delicious bagels, and drink a large container of Colombian roasted coffee. Now that's what I call breakfast!

That scene came to mind a few years later while I was interviewing Scotty Smith for this book. Scotty made the statement, "Prayer is like bread; I can go without it just so long," and for a moment my mind wandered back to those bagels—thinking how good they were to chomp into, warm and fresh and covered with all that wonderful, whipped cream cheese.

I know what Scotty means when he says that prayer is like bread. Bread is hearty; it satisfies us like nothing else. It's good for the body and the spirit. And it's best when it's made fresh daily. Prayer is all of those things too. And just as our stomachs can crave warm, fresh-baked bagels, so too is it possible to crave time in prayer with God—time when we speak, time when we listen, and time when silence is communication enough.

Some readers may ask, "What is prayer?" Prayer is our ongoing conversation with God. It can take place in a car, on a boat, or in a plane. Anywhere we can go, prayer can go with us. One of my favorite scriptures about prayer is Philippians 4:6, in which Paul instructs us, "Don't worry about anything; instead, pray about everything" (NLT). Most often we tend to stress the "don't worry" part of the verse. But let's focus on the other part for a moment: "Pray about everything." In essence, Paul is inviting us to join the 24/7 Prayer Club, whose members share their lives with God by talking with Him whenever they want about whatever is on their minds.

If you are new to the club, you may wonder how to get started. First, forget the misunderstandings that are pervasive in the Christian culture—for example, that the time to pray is in the morning or the evening or before a meal. You can pray at any time, and no time on the twenty-four-hour clock is more holy than another. Furthermore, there's no better place for God to hear your prayers than where you are right now. You may feel closer to God in a chapel, in the forest, or on a beach, but God is omnipresent, and He hears you best wherever you are. And you know that especially spiritual person in your circle who can really belt out a blessing? God doesn't expect you to pray like that person. He's much more concerned with your open heart before Him than your technique.

Second, when you pray, always be thankful for what God is doing in your life. Confess your sins to Him. (I prefer a child's terminology here: Tell Him the "bad stuff" that you do.) Ask Him for the things you need that are in His will for you. Remember, prayer changes us; it doesn't change God. We are being "tuned" to His likeness the way a piano is tuned to the proper pitch, and not the other way around. Yet in His amazing grace, God listens to our prayers and responds to them. And the more we experience that interaction, the more real and personal our faith becomes to us.

I'd say the oddest thing about prayer is that some Christians who know better still don't pray. "No time," they say, or, "Too busy." If this describes you, I want to encourage you to talk with God more and listen for God more. The stories in this chapter explore the ways that we can speak to God and listen for Him. Be inspired! As each of the authors has discovered, prayer is not a chore—it's a privilege. God owns everything in creation; He's smarter than everyone else; and best of all, He loves us. He wants what's best for us, and He has the know-how and the resources to make it happen. Who wouldn't want to talk every day with someone like that?

Some people excel in their spiritual lives by reserving a special time to be alone with God every day. They treasure that opportunity to pray, study the Word, and just be with the Lord. When life changes their schedule, they still find the time. Sheila Walsh is like that. She talks about her intimate time with God.

Sheila Walsh

My prayer life has changed since I've had a baby. I used to be very much a night person. I was not good in the morning, so I would always have my quiet time at night. Now I set my alarm and get up at 6:00 A.M. Between six and nine o'clock is my time. If our son wakes up before nine, as he usually does, my husband takes care of him. Those three hours are my time to be alone with the Lord, to pray, to read, to write, to study.

I think everyone has to find a time that is realistic for them. Life changes. We go through different seasons when different things apply. I discovered that while I used to love being with the Lord in the evening, I love it now in the morning. I love that quiet time at the beginning of the day before anything has happened. Before I've said hello to anyone else, I can meet with God and be with Him and focus my whole day through the filter of His love. Even when my son, Christian, is grown, I probably will keep up this morning habit, because I find it is best for me.

My favorite promise from God's Word is that if any of us lacks wisdom, we can ask God, and He will gladly give it. The one thing I am convinced of is that I lack wisdom! I don't have a clue. There have been times when a certain thing has seemed great to me, but further down the road I've wondered, *What were you thinking?* Now I think, *Why would you even try to get it right yourself? Why wouldn't you make it a habit to pray in every single situation?* So whether I'm going to a meeting, having a conversation like this one today—whatever I'm doing—I say, "Lord, You know me. I have no wisdom of my own, so I ask right now for Your words and Your wisdom." I pray continuously through the day, whenever I find myself facing situations in which I need His wisdom.

———

Here's a simple definition of prayer from Henry Blackaby: Prayer is God's invitation to us to stand in His presence and learn His heart.

Henry Blackaby

I discovered, as I was going through the Scriptures, that I needed to let the Scriptures guide me to an understanding of what prayer is and what its purpose is. And in that process I found that prayer is, preeminently, God's invitation to stand in His presence so that He can make known what He's up to, what's on His agenda, and what's on His heart, and adjust me in that time of prayer to Him. Many people get discouraged with prayer because they believe that prayer is God's provision for them to get anything from God that they ask. But I think they've got it reversed. To me, prayer is God's invitation to learn His heart and to make sure my life is on target with Him. Once I understand that purpose, I can begin to talk with God or listen to God about how He will provide.

Prayer is absolutely crucial to a Christian's life; it's how we get to know God, how we get to know what is on the heart of God. It's usually in a time of prayer that God makes major adjustments in our lives. Romans 8:26 says that one of our great weaknesses is that we don't know how to pray as we ought. But God has given us the Holy Spirit to help us in that incredible process of prayer. Often when I go to pray, I start in one direction and suddenly realize that my whole heart is moving to pray in another direction. That is the Holy Spirit saying, "Henry, you really didn't know what to pray, but at least you came to pray. Now I'm going to redirect you in your praying so that you will be dead-center in the will of God."

We went through a particularly critical time in our life when we learned that our sixteen-year-old daughter had cancer. I needed to know if there was something that God had in mind in that situation so that I could make the adjustments in my life and then guide our daughter and our family through it. As I prayed, John 11:4 became very real to me: "This sickness is not unto death, but for the glory of God, that the Son of God may be glorified by it" (NASB). My whole prayer life changed then to say, "Father, if You are going to be glorified in this, give me wisdom and understanding and counsel and power to go through it and make the right decisions. Help me to always be watching to see how You are going to be honored and glorified through this time." I thanked Him for the assurance that He gave me that my daughter's illness was not unto death.

She went through chemotherapy and radiation, but in the middle of it all, the doctors said, "We don't understand it, but we don't see any more cancer." It had been growing in her body for two years! In that situation, prayer and the Scriptures and the Spirit of God had guided us to know what was on the heart of God, how to adjust our lives, and how to be very, very alert to Him.

When our son took a wayward turn, it was in prayer that God directed me to know what to do, how to love him, how to forgive him, and how to adjust our lives so that God could work with him. And oh my, God has turned him around so radically! He once said, "I don't want to go to college; don't talk to me about it." He's now completing a Ph.D. He also said, "Don't talk to me about God's will," and now he is a pastor! So prayer is my very life. That's where I know the heart of God, and that's where I know how to adjust my life to Him.

We shouldn't try to learn a 1-2-3 method of prayer. Prayer can't be reduced to a formula! Instead, we should learn to listen for God's "still, small voice." It is in those quiet moments of prayer that we experience a deeper intimacy with our heavenly Father.

Tony Campolo

My prayer life has changed dramatically. I used to just read off a list of nonnegotiable demands to God, and that was my prayer life. But more and more, I wake up in the morning and I am just still and quiet; I say nothing to God.

Someone once asked Mother Theresa, "When you speak to God, when you pray, what do you say?" She answered, "I don't say anything. I listen." So the person said, "OK, when you pray, what does God say to you?" The answer was, "God doesn't say anything. God listens." Then she added, "If you don't understand that, I can't explain it to you."

I relate to that. That is exactly what my prayer life has become in the morning. I make my requests known to God in the evening, but in the morning I wake up, and I'm just still before God. It's like coming in out of the cold on a rainy night and sitting in front of a glowing fire. You just sit in front of the fire, and the warmth of the fire envelopes you and makes you feel so good; it turns you from misery to joy. When I go to prayer, I am just still before God. I let God love me and envelop me and penetrate my being. It's that experience of prayer that makes God very real to me.

———◆———

As Steve Brown knows, prayer brings us into greater intimacy with God. He shares about his own discovery of prayer.

Steve Brown

I wrote a book called *Approaching God* a couple of years ago at the request of a secular publisher. I said, "As if there are not enough books on prayer!" And they said, "No, they are all by experts. We want one by somebody normal."

I used to believe in God for the same reason I believe in the multiplication tables: If it's true, only stupid people ignore it. But at some point it became clear to me that while I knew theology and I was a Bible teacher and I prayed, people in the church where I was the pastor—people who didn't know theology and didn't know the Bible—knew God better than I knew Him. So I prayed something like, "God, my sin is more real to me than You are, and I want to know You in an intimate way." That was a heartfelt prayer. I had read Richard Foster's little book, *Celebration of Discipline,* and through that book started reading some of the contemplatives of the faith. I was beginning to learn to be quiet.

At about that same time I started waking up around four o'clock in the morning. At first I thought it must be because of my sin. Then I thought, *My sin isn't any worse than it was yesterday,* and I tried to go back to sleep but couldn't. So I got in the car, drove to my office, took a shower there, and began what has become a fifteen-year journey of seeing if prayer is real, if God is real.

Pagans don't pray because they are afraid God might be there and mess up their lives. Christians don't pray because they are afraid He might *not* be, so we do religious things instead. It is quite scary, especially if you are a pastor, to think that you might pray and not find God. Then you don't have a job. So it's better to do liturgy and religious stuff. But I was determined I was going to find out about prayer.

It's a weird thing. Sometimes when I've been the most sinful,

He loves me the most. When I've been the most obedient, He doesn't seem to come. I wrote one of the great books on prayer—and if you believe that, you will believe anything! But it is an honest book about some of the things I have learned. Sometimes my prayers seem empty, but a lot of times prayer is the central focal point of my life.

This past year we started a morning radio show. I get up at 3:30 in the morning and meet with the staff at about 4:30, and we start writing scripts and doing comedic stuff and planning what we're going to do on the program that day. The most significant loss of the last year has been the loss of that time with the Father in the morning. I really think I am doing what He wants me to do, but I can't tell you how much I miss that time! The program is going to become an afternoon program soon, and the thing I am looking forward to more than anything else is getting back those quiet moments.

———◆———

I once heard a pastor say that God's answers to prayer are like a traffic signal: Sometimes it's red, meaning "no"; sometimes it's yellow, meaning "go slow" or "not yet"; and sometimes it's green, meaning "go!" Though we may not always get the "light" we hope for, we can be sure that each answer to prayer comes from the wisdom of God and is intended for our best.

Frank Peretti

I don't think my knowledge of God is based on any specific experience; it's based on a life of trusting Him. He's proved in my own life

that He really is there, that He is the God who is true to His promises, and that He cares for me. After walking with Him for forty-plus
years, I don't have any trouble at all believing that He's there.

Generally speaking, I've found that the Lord answers prayers in
ways you're not expecting. He usually answers your prayers a lot
later than you think He should. But then it turns out to be just the
right answer time and time again. There have been a lot of times
when God didn't answer one of my prayers the way I thought He
should; but looking back, I'm really glad He didn't.

There was a girl that I really wanted to marry, but she dumped
me. I prayed so hard that the Lord would bring us back together
again, but He never did. Then I ended up marrying Barb and being
the happiest man I could ever be for the next twenty-seven years.
Every once in a while I think about that fervent prayer of mine:
"Oh Lord, I want to get back together again with so-and-so." Now,
I tell the Lord, "Oh dear Lord, thank You for not listening to me!
Thank You for not answering that prayer." Ever since then I've said,
"Lord, You're in charge. You make the calls. I trust You." I'm going
to let the Lord run things. He knows better about what's going on
than I do.

Prayer is largely conversational for me. It's an ongoing,
moment-by-moment conversation with the Lord. We talk all day
long, and especially when I'm writing. I try to make sure I'm in
tune with Him. There are those times when I get really down and
intense, and I do some real supplication prayer. I'm really crying
out to God for an answer or a need or some understanding. But
generally, I'm sitting there or lying on the couch or awake at night
or walking in the woods, and God and I will just talk, have a conversation. I'll just wonder about things, think about things, jot

down little notes, and thank the Lord when He helps me to figure things out.

———

We often find ourselves geared more toward action than toward talking to the Father. Even great men and women of God struggle with this tendency. With amazing frankness, Max Lucado addresses his own struggles with prayer.

Max Lucado

Sometimes I'm very good about sitting down and being quiet for an extended period of time, which for me is thirty to forty-five minutes. Other days, I'm not so good at it. I don't pray like I want to. I do have a specific time in the mornings when I try to have at least a few moments of reflection. But prayer is the single most difficult discipline of my life. I would rather work for God than talk to God—not because I don't believe in prayer, but because I'm not a very good pray-er. It's never come easy for me. It's a constant battle to say, "You know, it's more important that I talk to God about this than get to work on it." Prayer is not an area of my life that I would hold up as an example or model.

———

As we've said, prayer is a lifestyle—an ongoing conversation with God. That conversation can take place anywhere at any time. God is listening 365 days a year, twenty-four hours a day, seven days a week.

Scotty Smith

I do love to pray, but I want to dispel any notion that it means I must be up every morning at 4:00 A.M., on my knees in my closet. The man who mentored me for twenty-one years, Jack Miller, demonstrated for me the reality that prayer is a lifestyle. Prayer is simply an open-ended, ongoing conversation with God. Jack helped me realize that prayer is to be for the Christian like breathing. Literally, the more God-conscious I can live, the more I can know that God's heart is always a pursuing heart. I never have to get God's attention. He never leaves me or forsakes me. He is constantly delighting in His children, every one of His children. His favor rests upon us.

Jack helped me understand that the Father's heart is always there; therefore, the hours I spend in prayer include those closet times when I am simply alone with God. But just as importantly, they include those times when I'm walking through the mall and praying for people I see. They include times when I'm enjoying that trout on the end of my hook, when I'm thanking God that He made rainbow trout. And they include laments. Prayer is not just intercession; sometimes it's saying, "Lord, life is just too much right now."

Jack also helped me to look at the Book of Psalms and realize the full array of communication and communion registered in its pages. And looking at the whole Bible, we find God's sons and daughters showing great joy, great confusion—but always taking their argument to God. Therefore I think of a life of prayer as taking the argument; taking the anger; taking the praise, the joy, the longings, the fears, the hope—taking it all to the Father all the time.

That's how prayer has become more of a lifestyle for me, and with that, I've discovered the utter joy of praying with other believers. That joy has become more pronounced in my life since Jack's death three years ago, because he modeled the love and the joy, the passion and the feast of corporate prayer. For me, praying with my wife, praying with believers, praying with a group of international students in St. Louis—it has become like bread. Prayer has become bread. I can do without it only so long.

———

Many of us carry hurts and wounds from our pasts. Chonda Pierce talks about an amazing prayer experience that helped her to find healing for events that happened long ago.

Chonda Pierce

As human creatures on this side of heaven, I don't think we ever totally forget things from our past. It's not in our makeup. Our family had a little kitty cat that got hit by a car sometime ago. For a long time, whenever we'd drive past that spot on the corner, one of the kids would say, "Look, that's where Princess bit the dust." Eventually we moved away; but I know that if we took the ride down to Smyrna, Tennessee, and turned on the corner of Branford Drive and Lowry, one of our kids would say, "Look, this is the corner where Princess bit the dust."

I've experienced a lot of traumatic things in my life. I've been through times of Christian counseling to find healing, and I've spent time with a number of pastors to help sort out some of the issues. I felt that I was doing better, and I probably would have lived the rest of my life just fine; but something happened to me this year that was incredible. I experienced a prayer time that brought me an amazing emotional healing.

I spent several days talking with a prayer counselor about my life—my earliest recollection of my grandparents, my great-grandparents, anything I knew about my ancestral roots. After tracing all those things—everything I could think of about my family, myself, events good and bad—we talked it all out. I mean, it took days. It was incredible.

Then we began to pray. We prayed through my life. Some of the issues that came up, some of the sins of the past, I had already dealt with. I had known to go back and remind myself that they had been covered by the blood of Jesus. Those revelations were sweet reminders of the relationship I have with the Savior. But sometimes we forget that God forgets, and we continue to carry guilt. Then we can't figure out why we're miserable. We remind the Lord of our sin, and He hasn't got a clue what we're talking about because He forgave us a long time ago!

At one point, as I was talking about my childhood, I said, "We lived in this one house, and it was a really tough place. We were on food stamps, and life was hard. I remember Mama was gone a lot because she was working a second job, and Dad was gone. But a guy in our church thought my big sister was really talented, and he bought her a piano. And then we moved the piano to our next house—"

The counselor said, "Whoa, stop right there. Who was that man who bought the piano?" And I said, "Mr. McFarland—I think that was his name."

"Let's just stop and thank the Lord for him."

Suddenly I was aware of a tiny, little, lighted blessing in the midst of what I thought was a muck of mess. That was a sweet reminder of God's love.

For Chonda, God's peace is a critical element in life. She talks about her prayers for the gift of peace.

One of my favorite prayers is for God's peace to settle in. Sometimes when I'm sitting at my laptop and I need to write a book or whatever, I pray not so much for creative juices, but for peace. If I have peace settled across my shoulders, then the person God created to write this book will get it written! When that underlying current is flowing as gently as can be, then I do OK.

Peace is one of the sweetest gifts from God. I pray for peace for my children. I think that if they can have peace in their lives—a real, abiding peace—then the questions of their grades, their careers, who they're going to marry, are all settled. They're not as much of a worry when you have that sweet, abiding peace.

———

In prayer we find God's will for specific questions that are on our minds. Grant Jeffrey outlines how he seeks God's wisdom in the important issues of his life.

Grant Jeffrey

I've always felt that it is possible to know the will of God. It's strange to me that many Christians don't seem to know the will of

God in their life. God has said that if any man lacks wisdom, let him ask of God, who gives liberally.

The method by which my wife, Kay, and I find the will of God in our life is not through watching for open and closed doors, because that can be chancy. Some doors that are closed need to be broken down. Some doors that are open should not be gone through. That method can be too passive. When we want to find the will of God, we pray about something and research it. We make a list—all the pros for why we should do this, all the cons for why we should not. Then we pray intently and ask God to give us wisdom regarding this issue. We think about it, we discuss it, and we prioritize the list—the most important reasons pro and the most important reasons con. We rearrange, we eliminate, we add to.

Finally, after three or four days, we look at that list again, and we make a decision based on the wisdom that we believe God has given us in answer to our prayer. We decide pro or con, and then we check it. We say to God, "If we got our sums right, if we got the answer You want for us, give us a certitude, a quiet peace in our heart, that it's Your answer, Your will." When God has given both of us that peace, we proceed with the full knowledge that we are in His will. If on the other hand we are filled with doubt, we go back to the drawing board and go through the process again. It has not always been easy, but we have always known absolutely that we were in God's will when we followed His direction in this way.

———◆———

It's a "sound principle of psychology that men move toward what they want," says Brennan Manning. As Christians, we should want to spend time with Jesus above everything else, but that's not always the case. Part of our growing up in the faith is the constant reappraising of the things in our lives until knowing Jesus is what we value most.

Brennan Manning

Every morning I spend an hour alone with Jesus before breakfast, and every afternoon I spend an hour with Him before dinner. I call it conscientiously wasting time with Jesus. Hanging out with Jesus. Some days I call it "show up and shut up." But all in all, it's kind of a holy loitering. I think it's by our very nature that we spend time with people that we love. Love by its nature seeks communion. So it's not surprising that I would spend time with Paul Sheldon, because he's my friend. That's why I spend time with Jesus. If I'm not meeting Jesus on that level, then it's on a level of duty, obligation, rules, and regulations; sometimes I may do it, sometimes I may not.

It's a very sound principle of psychology that men move toward what they want. When I wake up in the morning, I don't say to myself, "You should have a cup of coffee." I want it, and I just go make it. If I don't have the desire to pray, I think it's much more honest to say, "Jesus, I really don't want to spend time with You. On my list of priorities, You are not number one. I am too caught up in my busyness—whether it's carving out my career, shaping my ministry, being with friends, or having time for play. I don't desire You above everything else. You are not the want in my life that transcends all other wants. It's very painful for me to admit that, but I know You prefer honesty above anything else. And so tonight, Jesus, I'm going to go to my bedroom. I'm going to lock the door. I'm going to kneel down, and I'm going to cry out to You, the God I half-believe in, for a baptism of fire, to move my 'should' to a want, to awaken passion within me—a fierce desire for an intimate, heartfelt relationship with You."

Why do I want an intimate, heartfelt relationship with Jesus? It goes back to a night I spent in a cave in the Sargasso Desert in Spain. I was living for months in solitude. I got up every morning at 2:00 A.M. for what we used to call in the old church "Nocturnal Adoration." I'd go to chapel in the cave and try to spend at least one hour in praise and thanksgiving. On the night of December 13, 1968, during what began as a lonely hour of prayer, I heard in faith Jesus Christ say, "For love of you, I left My Father's side, and I came to you—you who ran from Me, who fled from Me, who did not want to hear My name. For you, I was covered with spit, punched, beaten, and fixed to the wood of the cross."

That was more than thirty years ago. This morning, in an hour of quiet time right in this room, I realized those words are still burned on my life.

That night in the cave, there was a crucifix behind the altar. I looked at the crucifix for a long time and figuratively saw the blood streaming from every wound and pore in Christ's body. I heard the cry of His blood: "This isn't a joke. It is not a laughing matter to Me that I have loved You." The longer I looked, the more I realized that no man has ever loved me and no woman could ever love me as He does. I went out in the darkness and shouted into the night, "Jesus, are You crazy? Are You out of Your mind to have loved me so much?"

I learned that night what a beautiful man told me the day I went to seminary. I was twenty-three years old. He said, "Kid, you will not understand this now, but on the day you experience the love and the heart of Jesus Christ, nothing else in the world will ever again seem that beautiful or desirable."

What's the Secret?

Prayer is open, ongoing communication between God and us, His children. Spending time in prayer, conversing and communing with the heavenly Father who loves us, is like bread for our souls. Have you had a good meal lately?

Jesus Is the Treasure
We're Asked to Give Away

Digging around infield one day, a farmer cracks the blade of his shovel on the corner of a heavy wooden box buried just below the surface of the earth. He scrapes at the box and he digs deeper, his anticipation rising with each blade of dirt thrown aside. Finally he reaches the box, opens it, and finds inside something beyond his wildest dreams: treasure! There's one problem, however, and it's a big one. The farmer doesn't own the field. If he wants the treasure, he'll have to buy the land—and it will cost him everything he owns.

It's fascinating to see what lengths people will go to find treasure. Ever watch the Discovery Channel? Adventurers with sonar equipment, nautical maps, and underwater minisubs will sail to the ends of the earth and sweep the ocean floor yard by yard, searching for the wreckage of a three-hundred-year-old Spanish cargo ship they believe carried gold. The more distant the island on the ancient map, the deeper the sunken wreckage in the depths of the ocean, the shorter the window of opportunity, or the stormier the seas, the more irresistible, it seems, is the bounty.

The treasure found by the farmer in the parable, however, isn't priceless jewels, rare stones, or the lost gold of an ancient civilization. It's far more valuable than that. The treasure is God Himself, worth so much more than what the farmer (or you and I) is asked to pay for it—even though we're asked to give everything. This treasure is very special indeed; for like love, it can be given away and still retain all of its original value. You might say its value even increases.

Before Jesus returned to heaven, He commissioned His disciples to "go into all the world and preach the good news to all creation" (Mark 16:15). The disciples knew Jesus, and they recognized His identity as God. They had walked with the Treasure in the field. When Jesus commanded them to go and preach the good news, He was directing them into a sort of philanthropy—a giving away of treasure. The disciples began the first great dispersion of the good news of the gospel, a giving away that would thread its way into this century and lead to your and my reception of Christ.

When we share this treasure with others, we don't end up with less of it; we have more. And yet many of us who are finders of God's treasure couldn't be more confused about how to share the good news with others so that God's blessings can grow and multiply for all. We may feel inadequate, pushy, or just plain inept. Perhaps we don't fully grasp the significance of what we have found or its use for the greater good, or we underestimate the need that exists in the people around us. One thing is for sure: If we haven't learned a simple way to share this treasure with others—

one that makes sense to us, one that we're comfortable with—we're more likely to do treasure hoarding than treasure sharing.

For those of us who aren't called to preach, the most natural and effective way to tell others about the treasure is through living out the gospel in front of curious eyes. To do this requires our praying for others and being like Jesus in our relationships with others— being the honest one, the loving one, the kind one, the sacrificing one, the peacemaker, the friend, the servant. In that process we can tell our stories of God's eternal love lavished upon us.

You may be saying to yourself, "Isn't that the work of skilled pastors, trained professionals, and qualified, adventure-loving missionaries?" But of course, the job is too big for these people to carry out alone. Besides, we need the blessing and the benefit that come only from reaching out to others in love. Don't worry, you're going to love telling others about Jesus! It is one of those experiences in life when you feel like you're in exactly the right place, doing exactly the right thing. Let me give you an example.

A few years ago some friends and I went swimming after work. While we swam, the night descended, the stars came out, the underwater pool lights came on, and everything turned a translucent blue. When we got tired, we rested in the water and talked. One of the guys asked me what I was doing on Sunday. I told him that after church, I didn't have plans.

"After church? Do you *have* to go to church every Sunday?" another one asked. I don't want to make the moment seem more dramatic than it was, but I definitely felt all eyes upon me at that moment. Somehow the thin membrane that separates the spiritual world and the natural world had been cracked, and my friends wanted to peer over the divide into the world of faith to see what it was really like.

"No," I told them, "I don't have to go every Sunday, but I always do. I feel welcome there. We've got a great pastor, and I like hearing what he teaches. I like the atmosphere of just sitting in church, and I love the way I feel after the service."

They began firing questions at me—questions about faith, Jesus, and why I believe the Bible is true. They had a lot of misconceptions about the Bible and what it taught, but I just told them what I knew without feeling pressured to be the master of all theology. I explained the gospel as simply as I could. I needed a Savior to forgive me for the "bad stuff" I'd done, I told them, and I needed a Lord to direct my life. I'd lived with and without following God. Comparing the two lifestyles, I was now wise enough to understand which was best for me. And I told them that Jesus loved them, that He died for their sins too, and that they could have His gift of forgiveness and salvation.

Clink, clank. More shovels hitting something buried beneath the surface. Would they find the treasure?

The guys were so open. We talked for almost an hour, and afterward one of the guys came up and thanked me for my candor. It was obvious to me that he was being impacted by the gospel. Another one of the men went with me to a local crusade in south Florida and raised his hand when the audience was given an opportunity to accept the Lord that night. (Tony Campolo was the main speaker.) I visited the third man in his home one evening, and he was excited to show me a puzzle he'd found—one of those which, when you looked at it a certain way, reveals the name "Jesus." I knew that he was at least thinking about the Lord.

So often the inquiry of skeptics uncovers the hunger in their hearts. I'll never forget that night in the pool, but there have been other, similar times. I love talking about my faith in Christ because it's exciting to me. I don't need to hold a Ph.D. to share Jesus, and neither do you.

In this chapter I asked the authors to tell how they approach sharing Jesus with others. I hope their stories will encourage you to speak more candidly about your faith. After all, Jesus is the treasure we're asked to give away—and it's a wonderful thing to give something so valuable to the people we know and love.

Henry Blackaby has pastored churches for three decades. What, I wondered, is his counsel to those who are seeking God?

Henry Blackaby

I have pastored for about thirty years. I always try to use the Scripture to help people who are seeking to understand that what is happening in their life is the activity of God. For instance, if a person says that he is really seeking after God but doesn't know the direction to go, I would say, "Let me take you to Philippians 2. The scripture says, 'Let the implication of your salvation work itself into every area of your life, because it is God who is at work in you causing you to do His will and then enabling you to do it.'" I would stop and share with him that he would never be seeking after God unless God was initiating that search in his heart.

Then I would take him to another scripture and say, "You just told me you were really seeking after God. Romans 3:11 says that because of sin, nobody seeks after God, and nobody understands. But here is a scripture that says that if you do find yourself seeking after God, it is God who is at work within you causing you to want to seek Him. Do you believe that?" Next I would counsel him to stay in the Scriptures and let the Spirit of God show him from the Scriptures what God is up to in his life. When you know that it is God who is at work in you, when you have the incredible understanding of the implications of having the God of the universe guide you, you begin to have God-sized things unfold in your life.

I would take that person to the Scriptures again and say, "Here's what happened in Peter's life when God put it in his heart to follow Jesus. That opened up a whole new life for Peter. Then God shaped him to know God and to walk with God one day at a time. Would you be willing to let God shape you one day at a time?" Sometimes a person says, "Oh, I wish I could understand the Bible like you do." And I say, "You have the same teacher I do, and that's the Holy Spirit. But I've been letting the Holy Spirit guide me for years and years, so I have a backlog of a great walk with God in which He's been so faithful."

I tell a person who's on the front end of the process, "Don't be discouraged because you're around someone who has a mature walk with God. That walk comes one day at a time, and there's no short-cut to it. There's no six-step lesson to hearing the voice of God. Just be content to be a young believer and let God guide you one step at a time. Five years from now you'll be a lot further along than you are today, and ten years from now you'll be amazed at the difference God has made.

"So use the Scriptures, trust the Spirit of God to guide you, and apply the things you learn to your life personally. Don't be afraid to take baby steps as you learn the process of walking with God. Don't ever hurry that process. But know that you can experience the fullness of God at the point at which you understand Him right now."

As a pastor, I wouldn't just tell that person the truths of the Scriptures. I would do what Jesus said: teach him to practice, to live out in his life, everything Christ has commanded. I'd encourage him to stay in the Gospels and learn who Jesus is and how He relates and how He responds to the Father, because God has placed Jesus in that person's life. "He's going to be living out His life in you," I'd say. "You need to know Him!"

———

If we are overzealous in our delivery of the gospel, we can degrade the very message that we represent. Brennan Manning emphasizes the importance of allowing seekers to ask questions first before we offer answers.

Brennan Manning

The seeker has come to me. I didn't go to him. Or the seeker has come to the church. So it begins not with trying to convert the person by concussion—with one sledgehammer blow of the Bible after another until he falls down and says, "Save me! Save me from *you*, you nut. You are a fanatic." It begins with me asking, "Why are you here? What are you seeking? Why are you restless? Do you feel there's got to be more to life than what you are experiencing?

"If that's the case—if you are seeking something you don't

have—the very pragmatic question is, Could the more that you are seeking be God? And would you like to investigate this further? Would you be willing to spend an hour with me each week, and together we'll explore your hunger, your longing, your emptiness, your need? We'll see if the God revealed in Jesus meets that need. You know, you've got a lot of company. St. Augustine said, 'Our hearts are restless until they rest in God.' So, welcome to the club of the restless."

I asked Brennan what he thinks keeps so many Christians from sharing about their faith in Jesus.

The failure of Christians to evangelize is an inexcusable lack of compassion. The ministry is motivated by compassion for people who don't have a clue who Jesus is or who have terribly distorted images of God—caricatures that bear no resemblance to the God embodied in Jesus of Nazareth. Our goal is to present the God of Jesus, who, as John writes in his first letter, is love, and to move people out of the house of fear and into the house of love.

———

Either through the spoken word or through print, Max Lucado's gift is expressing the gospel. Max gives insights on how we can share the gospel by living our faith well in front of others.

Max Lucado

I think the most important thing is a life well lived. I believe a person living an honest life, a life of good character, good integrity; who loves his spouse; who does his work well, shows up on time, pays the bills—that's the gospel in the flesh. Anybody can learn to quote verses or teach a gospel story, but not everybody can lead a quality life and be an example.

I've played golf for about seven years now at the same golf course with a man who is not a Christian. Not too long ago he said, "You know, Max, everybody at this country club knows who you are, and they like you anyway!" I felt very good about that. They know I'm a preacher, but they like me anyway. If you can lead a life in your neighborhood in such a way that they know you're a Christian, but they like you anyway—that, I think, is the power of the gospel.

———

When it comes to sharing our faith, Steve Brown doesn't believe in beating people over the head with the gospel; he says we're called to cast our line into the sea of humanity around us and wait to see if somebody "bites."

Steve Brown

As Christians we are in the business of answering the questions that our lives have produced in the lives of others. I have this principle that you don't share the gospel with somebody who does not want to hear it. But let's assume that a seeker has been drawn by the Spirit and warmed by the fire of the church or of Christians, or in some way feels very empty or sees a great need; he or she has become an illustration of the statement from Augustine that God has "created us for thyself, and our hearts are restless until they find their rest in thee."

Generally, with people like that, I would sit down and talk about their hunger. I would talk about the way hunger presupposes food, thirst presupposes water, and this hunger that Blaise Pascal describes as a "vacuum" presupposes a God that sits in the God-shaped vacuum. I would then take them as far as they wanted to go in terms of the details. If God's Spirit was working in them, I would talk about sin and what it does to them—how it separates them from themselves, from other people, and, most importantly, from God. I would talk about the holiness of God and how they don't want to tick Him off—and how they already have. I would talk about the fact that they are going to have to stand before Him someday. And then I would present, as simply as I could, what happened on the cross, how Christ died vicariously for our sins. The Lamb was slain on our behalf. I would talk about the atonement and about the importance of making that personal in their life. Then I would ask them to pray with me.

That's a fairly traditional presentation of the gospel. I might even use the "Roman Road" or the "Four Spiritual Laws" or something similar. But I would presuppose that God's Spirit is working in their life, and I would try to be sensitive to the working of His Spirit. Wherever we are, I think we're called to cast lines over the side to see if the fish are biting. We're not called to try to reach down over the water, hit them with a bat, and drag them in. Every day we have opportunities to cast a line over and see if somebody wants to bite. And if someone wants to hear our story, we've got a wonderful one, and it's true.

———

The Holy Spirit helps us put into words a message that will impact others. Comedian Chonda Pierce tells how the Holy

*Spirit helps her communicate the gospel on stage and how it's OK
to adapt, not the message, but our presentation of the message.*

Chonda Pierce

When I perform, I know the funny stories I want to tell and the
direction that I want to go in. I've worked on this material, and I
hope it's funny. So I go out onstage, and nine times out of ten,
something happens, and I write more comedy standing there in
front of the people. The Holy Spirit does breeze through a room,
helping you with what's coming out of your mouth and what's going
into the ears of somebody sitting there. I see that happen before my
very eyes. When I see someone being touched, I know it isn't me,
because I'm just this kid from a little town in Tennessee!

When my pastor is in the pulpit, and he's got a sermon that the
Lord laid on his heart, and he is, as we say in comedy, "on a roll,"
it's obvious that the Holy Spirit is at work. If you go out and eat
lunch with him when church is over, he's a different person. I can't
imagine eating supper with Max Lucado and the conversation
around the table being a beautiful story about the robe of Christ.
I'm sure he doesn't phrase things at the dinner table with his kids
the way he does in a book. When Jesus was sitting out in an open
field with five thousand hungry people at His feet, I imagine He
talked a little bit louder than He did when He was sitting across the
table having lunch with Zacchaeus. We all adapt. We adapt every
day to wherever it is that He puts us. Our body language and our
voice inflections change. Part of being God's creature is being able
to adapt to where you are.

Do you remember the movie It's a Wonderful Life, *starring Jimmy Stewart and Donna Reed? In the film Stewart's character, George Bailey, receives the extraordinary gift of seeing what would have happened in the lives of his loved ones had he never been born. I asked Frank Peretti what his life might have been like had he never had an encounter with Christ.*

Frank Peretti

Well, let's see. I'd be divorced, probably. I'd be miserable and disillusioned. I don't know if I'd be into any kind of substance abuse. I might have a venereal disease by now! What's kind of funny about this is that I can't even imagine not being a Christian. I think eventually I would have come to Christ, because I would have wanted answers to the big questions of life. It amazes me when I meet people who don't seem to care about their eternal destiny, who don't seem to ask the big questions. They just plod through life, working through the week and going out drinking on the weekends. I'm like, don't you even care about why we're here and where we're going and how we should live?

I have always cared about the big stuff. So if I had not been born into a Christian home, I may have gone around looking into all kinds of different philosophies. I may have tried Eastern mysticism or some other weird religion, but I think I would have found Christ eventually. I can't imagine Frank Peretti, given his personality and his mentality, not coming to Christ eventually.

We're responsible to share the love of Christ with others, to be an encouragement to them, and to show them by example who we believe in. If we show people only what we're against, how will they come to understand Jesus, the gentle Savior who serves us in humility and unconditional love?

Sheila Walsh

I travel with five other women in a team called Women of Faith, and we go around the country speaking on different themes each year. The first year our theme was joy; another year we talked about grace. We've talked about all sorts of different subjects. But the joke inside the team is that it doesn't matter what subject we're on; Sheila will talk about the love of God. That's true! To me, grace, truth, hope, freedom, and peace make no sense outside the context of the love of God. How can you possibly understand grace if you don't understand the love of God?

Unfortunately, I think the church in America is identified by what we stand against. Ask some normal, unchurched people to describe an evangelical Christian. They'll say, "Well, they're people who hate homosexuals, who hate this or hate that, who stand against this or stand against that." But we should be people who are known for standing for something powerful: the unconditional love of God. We think it's our responsibility to tidy up the world. That's not our responsibility! Our responsibility is to love the world and invite people to come to the feet of Christ; and if there is any cleaning up to do, He will do it. It's not our job!

It is so wonderful when you are just beginning to embrace the possibility that there is a God out there who really loves you. Sometimes you have to get rid of all the stuff that's not true before you can embrace what is true. A lot of people think, *If there is a God,*

I'm not sure I would want to know Him. Look at the mess everything is in. Look at the mess in my own life. Look at all the bad things that have happened. I have talked to people who've said, "I shot out a couple of quick prayers and asked God, 'If You are out there, then get me out of this jam or do this thing for me.' He didn't, so maybe there isn't a God."

What I tell people to do is to just open their heart to God and say to Him, "I don't have a clue who You are. I don't even know how I'm supposed to do this. But if it is true that You are out there, if You are the one who put me together, then I would like to know You. I don't have a clue where You live, but You know where I live. So please show up in ways that will make sense to me, and let me know who You are."

When I was a little girl, my aunt gave me an old, very beautiful watch. One night I decided to take it apart to see how it worked. I completely ruined the thing. I couldn't get all the pieces back together, and I was so upset. I finally got the courage to go to my mom and say, "Look, I've ruined this watch." She said, "No, it's probably not ruined, darling. If you have all the parts, we'll take it to a watchmaker."

I would say the same thing about life. So often we feel our life is a mess, and we try to get it all together and tidy it up before we bring ourselves to God. I tell people, don't bother doing that. Bring yourself to the Watchmaker. Bring yourself, with all your broken pieces, to the One who made you in the beginning, because He knows where every piece goes. No matter what your life is like, no matter how awful you think you've been, the one thing I know as deep as the marrow in my bones is that God loves you.

Staying spiritually sensitive to those who are hurting around us can open up opportunities for us to pray for them. Not only can we show Christ's love in their time of need; we may find ourselves being blessed as well.

Patsy Clairmont

When it comes to interacting with people, I think some of the funniest and best things have happened on airplanes. Of course, the most fun I have on an airplane is getting off. I'm just so glad to be wherever I'm going so I can get on with what I'm there to do! But at some point I realized, what if the most important thing God gave me to do on a trip was to be involved with someone on the airplane, and I missed that chance?

I remember getting on a plane one time and seeing a little girl get on after me who was evidently being flown from one parent to another. She was very sorrowful; her face was exceedingly sad, and she also looked angry. She was probably about eight years old. They sat her next to a mother who had a child with her, and that child was immediately very friendly and warm and tried to draw the little girl into conversation. But the girl would have no part of it. Then the mother tried to talk to the girl, but the girl refused to respond. She didn't want to look at them, much less speak to them. Her lips were tight, her little arms were folded across her chest, and she seemed determined to be miserable.

I began praying for her. I was seated in a way that when she looked up, she was looking right at me. I reached in my purse, found a piece a gum, and began praying that somehow I could communicate without words and break through to this little girl. She looked up at me and I looked at her, and I let a little smile slip across my lips as I lifted up that piece of gum. She looked at me for a moment, then nodded her head to indicate she would receive it. So with her permission, I entered her little circle of reference, gave her that piece of gum, and watched as she totally relaxed and opened up. She began talking with the child next to her, then to the child's mother, all the while looking over and smiling at me. She had had a breakthrough! I really believe it was the Lord's assignment for me that day to pray for that little girl, to help bring her out of a very dark little spot.

I think that many times we deny ourselves an opportunity to be used by God and to be blessed by God because we don't like what we're having to walk through. I was blessed by the opportunity to pray for that little girl. I saw God change not only her countenance but her whole sense of security. It was very sweet to my soul, and it has stayed with me.

What do you see when you look at the people around you? Sharing the treasure of the gospel starts with recognizing the incredible value God places on every one of us.

Larry Crabb

The popular phrase for years has been "friendship evangelism." It's a good phrase. C. S. Lewis wrote a marvelous article called "The Weight of Glory." In essence he says that when you look at your neighbor cutting the lawn or see a person checking out groceries at the supermarket—I'm using my words, not his—you're looking at someone who, if you could see them in their eternal state, would either cause you to want to almost fall down and worship or back away in horror. People are that significant. I like the Francis Schaeffer phrase, "no little people." You need to look at people as ones who bear the image of God, who are profoundly valuable. Your message is not to judge them, to get them to stop smoking, to get the rings out of their ears, or even to get them to stop having affairs. That isn't the message. God is not looking to moralize the world. God is looking to restore the world to Himself, and the result will be morality.

We make the mistake in our witnessing of simply confronting the world with all the bad things and blasting them with the truth of the gospel—"You're going to hell; here's the plan of salvation," rather than, "You're a valuable image-bearer. Let me be interested in you; let me explore who you are and where you are." People are so desperately hungry for someone who cares, for someone who's interested. When's the last time you told a story and people listened to you all the way through? I mean, who gives a rip when you tell somebody that you've been to the hospital? Nobody's interested in hearing the details for half an hour. I'm convinced that if we learn to appreciate people and take them seriously, our success in personal evangelism will double.

———————

In sharing our faith with children, it is not enough to simply tell the gospel. We must live it before them. Karyn Henley offers

*a great lesson for parents who want to know how to teach their
children about Jesus.*

Karyn Henley

There is definitely a hunger among parents for information.
"We have certain values," they say, "but how do we communicate
our values to our children? We know there is a kingdom of darkness
and a kingdom of light, and we see what happens to kids when we
don't communicate effectively. How do we keep our children in the
kingdom of light?"

These questions are especially significant as we see revival beginning to take place. Many parents themselves are moving out of the
kingdom of darkness and into the kingdom of light. They are committed to the Lord, but they had no models in their growing-up years
showing them how to be good parents. They are in the new kingdom,
but they were never taught how to train their children. The need is
great to show adults who are being discipled and loved into the kingdom of light how to communicate God's love to their children.

We must do four things to communicate the gospel to children.
The first is to pray. Always pray, whether you are an old Christian or
a new Christian. Pray for your kids, because God needs to make up
for your deficiencies as a parent. We all have deficiencies, and we
need to pray. The second thing is to play. That may seem like a
strange thing to say, but playing with our kids is the foundation for
building a relationship. And when you build a relationship, the door
is opened for effective communication. You play with young children in a different way than you play with older children, of course,
but you play with kids!

The third thing is to act to be copied, and the fourth thing is to speak to be echoed. Kids will do both. They will copy you and they will echo you, so you need to pay attention to the way you act and the way you speak. So pray, play, act to be copied, and speak to be echoed. It sounds simple, but when you try to incorporate these four things into your daily life, you'll find it's very hard. But it's a good goal.

Many of the lessons we learned early in life came from watching what our parents did. Children imitate what they see growing up, and in that way they very often inherit their parents' faithfulness, creativity, and compassion for others.

Grant Jeffrey

I was born into a Christian family. From the time I was a very young child, I had exposure to Christ in the love my parents had for each other and for Christ. When I was eight years old, I came forward at a Youth for Christ meeting in Ottawa and gave my heart to the Lord. I can remember as early as ten and eleven witnessing to my friends. My folks were involved in church and Sunday school, and by the time I was seven, they had bought an eight-hundred-acre ranch about sixty miles west of Ottawa. We had more than one hundred quarter horses. The idea was to have a camp for unsaved kids where the counselors would be Christian. We would not preach at them, but we would try to share our faith in Christ by one-on-one personal evangelism. Over thirty years, thousands of boys and girls were saved at that camp, which we called Frontier Ranch.

It was a marvelous experience growing up hunting, fishing, training horses, riding, and working with kids on that property. I started as a camper and then worked as a counselor, a program director, and in other roles. I call my company Frontier Research because of the fond memories I have of that camp. My dad used the profits from his company, Jeffrey Luggage, to in effect subsidize the camp. That is what inspired me to form my own company. Frontier Research is not set up as a charity that asks for donations. Instead, I ask the Lord to bless our sales so that we can support our ministry and never ask for funds.

Out of the profits from the sale of the books, we fund our ministry travels to Singapore, Kenya, and around the world. We fund all our donations to missionaries from the book sales. We give away thousands and thousands of books to prisoners in the United States and in Canada. It has really given us a tremendous freedom. Unlike most ministries that spend half their time on fund-raising letters and campaigns, God has given us an ability to spend 100 percent of our time on research, writing, and getting the books in the hands of people around the world.

———

A prerequisite to encouraging someone else to follow Jesus is having a relationship of our own with Christ. As we share with gentleness what has happened along our own faith journey, we find that our dialogue conveys the message that Jesus meant for us to carry.

Scotty Smith

Fortunately we are at a time in our culture when spiritual interest, spiritual hunger, is surfacing in a very refreshing way. If I met a man or woman who was asking good questions, I would want to start by simply saying, "Tell me your story. I want to hear about your longings, your fears, your joys. I want to hear about what's driving your life. I want to listen to your heart. I want to know the images of God that have been set up in your heart, by whatever means; and don't hold anything back from me. Don't feel a need to present God to me in a way that will make Him look sanitized or keep from offending me. I want to make sure that I understand you; because what you think, what you feel, and what you believe really does matter to me."

I would enjoy listening, and then I'd say, "I would love the privilege of sharing my story as well. We have a lot in common. We're both thirsty, we're both hungry, and we're both needy. Let me share my journey of how the God of all grace has revealed Himself to me. He has confronted me in my fears, my brokenness, my longings, my foolish mistakes; and He has dismantled many wrong images I had of Him. I used to think of Him as an indifferent, distant Father. I used to think of Him as a cosmic killjoy who wanted to find out what I liked to do just so He could say no.

"I've had images of God that were grounded not in the God who is, but in the God of my experience, the God of my culture, the God of people I grew up with. The real God needed to cut through all of that. He needed to dismantle those images, and He lovingly did. I hope that my story and your story intersect in such a way that as you hear how He has made Himself known to me, you will want to dialogue further. Then I can listen more to that part of your heart that really wants to know Him."

When we come to Christ and begin to follow His lead, all the price tags in our lives get switched. Things we once considered so valuable that we thought we couldn't live without them no longer seem important to us. Meanwhile, the things we never cared for much become priceless.

I asked Scotty to talk about the currencies of our lives.

To think of the pearl of great price and the treasure hidden in the field is to realize that there are many different currencies in life. I need to decide which currency is going to be the one that consumes me. Which currency do I want to live with in this world—the currency of dollars or the currency of truth, the currency of grace, the currency of freedom, the currency of integrity? This is such a short life; what does it mean to be a steward of my brief moment between the comings of Christ? The price tags change. As Paul says in Philippians 3, "That which I used to value so highly I now consider as loss compared to the majesty, the glory, the unsurpassable riches of knowing Christ Jesus my Lord."

What's the Secret?

Jesus is the Treasure in the field. We need to claim that treasure for ourselves—and then give it away with joy.

Secret #9

We All Need the Savior, Jesus

I want to visit Great Britain at least once during my lifetime. From the photographs I've seen of the UK and in the movies I've watched that were filmed in London, I'm convinced of its unequaled beauty and grace in all the world. To me, the majestic landscapes of Scotland and Northern Ireland and the hospitality and charm of the British people hint at what heaven must be like.

We each have a place that we dream of—a site of peace and tranquillity, a pleasing escape from all our worldly concerns. The mysterious attraction of that beautiful and enchanting place beckons us when we're stymied by the challenges of the here and now. But far from fantasy, England is a very real place; and simply knowing that it's real elevates my spirit.

There's also a person who elevates my spirit when I face difficulty. His name is Jesus; and every time I think of Him, my mind remembers His unequaled beauty and majesty. My spirit can't help but rise because, like England across the Atlantic, He is not a mere fantasy. Knowing that He's real calms the storms in my life.

We all need the Savior, Jesus, because we are a people in need of salvation. When our private and public worlds stir up issues and challenges, crises and confusion, we need to know that our comfort rests in keeping our eyes on the Prince of Peace. When the evening newscast leaves us spinning with vertigo, we need to remember the one who holds the world steady in His hands. When the morning newspaper reads like a rap sheet—telling tales of crime, tragedy, suffering, and bloodshed—we need to turn to the only One who can write peace into our fearful and worried hearts.

Jesus is the solution for all the problems in our world; He's the answer for all the issues that most concern us. Simplistic? Yes. But is it complexity we're looking for or a simple Savior who has the power to free us, restore us, and heal us? To say that Christ possesses great power is the ultimate understatement. Jesus isn't challenged by the confusing upheaval of our restless and careworn lives. It is nothing to Him to vanquish the foes that threaten and entrap us.

Sometimes anxiety sprouts from circumstances in the world around us, and sometimes it grows from the inside out. In those latter times we feel artless, unable to manage and unwilling to change the frail lives we lead. We seem unable to follow the moral teachings we've heard all our lives. We aren't consistently good, even by our own scant standards, and we fail at trying to be good more often than we'd like to admit. We break God's law (and His heart) by choosing things other than Christ to satisfy us—yet none do.

Despite our failures, Christ's offer to us stands: He will forgive us of our past misdeeds, establish us in a right relationship with the Father, and teach us His ways to replace all our broken, faulty ones.

Do we believe Him? Do we believe in Him? Jesus will straighten out our issues if we'll hand the problems over to Him. He is the Living Water that saturates our parched and brittle lives. His forgiveness changes us from unacceptable to perfect, and, over time, from broken to whole. As dramatic as winter giving way to spring, the ice melts away from us with His touch, and the seed He's planted in our hearts becomes green, alive, and growing.

Don't know how to begin repairing the damage in your life? James 1:5 states, "If any of you lacks wisdom, he should ask God, who gives generously to all without finding fault, and it will be given to him." Can't shake free from guilt buried deep in the past? First John 1:9 says, "If we confess our sins, he is faithful and just and will forgive us our sins and purify us from all unrighteousness." Have a problem you think no one can solve? Jesus says, "Until now you have not asked for anything in my name. Ask and you will receive, and your joy will be complete" (John 16:24).

We each have concerns that weigh heavily upon our minds, be they outer world or inner space, health or wealth, poverty or politics. All of the authors I interviewed have concerns too. In this chapter they voice some of those concerns about our world, our nation, and the church in America. But they are not anxious or discouraged; they have found the answer. As you and I confront the problems that threaten us, let us consider the faultless man whose very identity is the solution: Jesus. Would our problems seem so insurmountable if we gave them over to His lordship—if we simply trusted Him more?

In asking the authors what concerns them most, I didn't expect "success" to top anyone's list. However, when I asked Steve Brown what most concerned him about the church in America, he made an interesting point: As Christians we can succeed at something without Jesus—and lose what God has for us in the process.

Steve Brown

My concern is that we, the church, would be successful. Now, I'm very conservative politically and theologically, and I support the issues of the Religious Right. But I'm afraid that at some point we may get too successful or too powerful in the political arena. My mentor, Fred Smith, says that whenever the government hooks the church, the church always hooks back. When we can deliver votes, the government will hug us, and we will hug back. I think if we get too powerful and too good at it, we will have found a way other than Christ's way to do our work. So my concern is that we will constantly work to do things the world's way, be successful at it, and lose what God has given us.

Even though we love God, we are always in danger of becoming "consumer Christians" who believe God exists only to serve us. How can we truly serve others if our own hearts long to be served?

Scotty Smith

One of my favorite authors is J. I. Packer, who wrote the classic volume *Knowing God.* Being from Great Britain, he was asked, "Dr. Packer, what do you think of American piety?" In a very humble, loving, and tender way he said, "Well, certainly there are a lot of wonderful things to be encouraged about; but by and large, I see it as three thousand miles wide and three inches deep."

Certainly that metaphor can be defined and understood in many ways. I see American spirituality being superficial and not very deep in the "consumer spirit" of our day. We are a consumer-driven culture, and I find many times in our churches, Christian literature, and Christian media an unspoken assumption that God exists to make my life more enjoyable. He exists to make my life more cope-able. He's there to come through for me. Consumerism basically asks the question, "What's in it for me?"

I long for my heart, the hearts of our church members, and the hearts of this generation to experience revival. Revival would get us back to the notion held by the Christians in the eighteenth century, those who put together the Westminster Shorter Catechism and framed that first great question: "What is the chief end of man?" Their response was, "The chief end of man is to glorify God and to enjoy Him forever." I would love to see my heart and the hearts of our church and this generation of Christians brought back to an other-centered experience of the gospel—an experience in which we truly can say with joy, "I exist just to bring glory and pleasure to God. I enjoy it, and I get great benefits out of it; but those things are secondary to the joy I have of simply being His son, His daughter, being involved in the advancement of His kingdom."

Compare that to the modern attitude that basically says, "You know, God owes me. He didn't answer my prayers because I prayed for a spouse, and here I am, forty-eight and still single." I fully identify with anyone who sits in the brokenness and longing of unanswered prayer. But the point is that this culture has a consumer-driven nature that concerns me. I pray that God would be pleased to arrest this drive and bring us to a place of real freedom in Him.

———

Christians often lay the blame for society's moral decline at the feet of the non-Christian world. However, just as the prophets rebuked God's people in times of old, we are the ones being admonished today for failing to lead others by His example.

Brennan Manning

I would say a divided body of Christ is probably the most painful thing to look at in terms of the church—the childish bickering among the denominations and nondenominations, the prejudice that many of us seem to have inherited with our mother's milk, the distrust between Catholics and Protestants, the longstanding biases, the terrible misunderstandings of one another's doctrine and belief systems. These are the things that have caused enormous problems. Wars are fought over this kind of stuff!

It's painful to look at how we've denied Jesus, since the only witness that He asked for was His love. He said, essentially, "You're going to be known as My disciples not because you are chaste, celibate, honest, sober, respectable; not because you are churchgoing, Bible-toting, and psalm-singing. You'll be identified by one sign only: your deep and delicate respect for one another, your cordial love and respect for the sacred dimension of every personality." Jesus said, "You'll be known as Mine by the way you love one another."

What Jesus was saying is that discipleship is all about loving. It is not about worship and morality, except insofar as worship and morality are expressions of the love that causes them both. A loveless liturgy, a loveless act of worship, is a meaningless liturgy in the sight of God. A loveless marriage, a loveless celibate life, anything without love, as Paul says, is nothing but sounding brass, a tinkling cymbal.

I believe in the days that lie ahead in the twenty-first century, a person is either going to be a mystic or nothing at all. By a "mystic" I mean someone who has experienced something. I don't mean Christians who believe that Christianity is a moral code or a philosophy of life. I mean Christians who know it is a love affair. The immense and tender love of God is experienced in the bowels of their very being. When persecution comes—and it will—those who survive, those who cling to Jesus, will be those who have really experienced Him.

———

Tony Campolo is encouraged that Christians are getting more politically involved, becoming a voice on important issues, and representing the truth of God in the public arena. He warns us, though, not to become captive to any one political ideology.

Tony Campolo

An encouraging thing has been happening in America: The American Christian community has become very aware that relevant Christianity requires political involvement. The thing that scares me, though, is that many Christians have allowed themselves to become partisan in their politics. It is very important for Christians to speak out on social issues; but I think it is very dangerous when all the Christians show up at the annual meeting of one party or the other.

I worry about the partisan nature of politics that is emerging in

America. I think it can lead us to great disaster. As Christians we must stand above political institutions and parties and speak the Word of God to both parties. We must declare the truth of God as we read it and as we understand it to people on both sides of the political aisle. We must not allow ourselves to become captive to either side.

———

Sheila Walsh grew up in a small village in Scotland and now makes her home in the United States. Given her unique perspective, it's interesting to hear what concerns her about her adopted country.

Sheila Walsh

One of the things that concerns me about America is how we make money based on people's fear. You can see this even in some of the current titles in Christian bookstores. We are so obsessed with money and success that when we see a chink in people's armor, we hone in on that spot and look to make money by capitalizing on their fear about it. But doing something based on fear has nothing to do with the heart of God. What kinds of lessons are we teaching our children about what is important, what is valuable, what is a successful life?

I think of someone like my Aunt Mary in Scotland who is eighty-five and still lives by herself in the same small house, still cuts her own firewood. When Aunt Mary is gone, she will be greatly missed because of the legacy of faith she has left, because of her quiet wisdom through the years, and because of what she has taught everyone in our family about courage through difficult times and perseverance through pain. To me, that's a successful life.

We named my son "Christian" after the character in one of my favorite books, *The Pilgrim's Progress* by John Bunyan. One of the things I want to teach Christian is that life is a journey, and it is not all uphill. I want to tell him, "When you find yourself on the other side of a hill, when you find yourself falling, that doesn't mean that God has left you. If you just keep walking and keep your faith and keep holding Christ's hand, you will have lived up to your name." That will be success.

When salt loses its saltiness, it no longer preserves. When the light gets dim, it no longer disperses the darkness. Henry Blackaby reminds us that we are our nation's salt and light, and we hold the key to America's future.

Henry Blackaby

I think we're on the edge of the judgment of God, and the key to that is God's people. God's people, however, are not yet aware that they hold the key to the future of America. We need to understand that our problem is not with the darkness; the darkness is simply acting according to its nature. The problem is with the light. The light is not dispersing the darkness. Our problem is not that things around us are rotting; they're just acting according to their nature. The problem is that the salt that should be preserving America has lost its saltiness.

If we do not see a mighty return of the people of God back to a vital relationship with God, I believe God will judge the nation. And when He does, it will be thorough and radical. I think we're standing on the edge of that right now. I look at the message of 2 Chronicles

7:14, which is the heart cry for revival. In this passage God addressed His people. His people held the key to the healing of the land. "You need to pray, you need to seek My face, you need to turn from your wicked ways," He said. "Then the first thing I will do is forgive your sin. Next, I'll heal your land." It is useless to ask God to heal our land if we are not willing to follow the prerequisites that are required for God to do it.

When I walk among God's people, it seems that they don't even know they've departed from God. But the people of God must be preeminently a people of prayer, because God in 1 Peter 2:9 says, "You are…a royal priesthood." In other words, the people of God, by nature, are to be people who pray. And yet when you look at the family life of God's people, the personal walk of God's people, and the church life of God's people, you see that prayer is not a major factor. Look at the bulletins of many churches. You don't see much in the area of prayer. You see aerobics, sports, cancer recovery, divorce recovery, but you don't see prayer. Yet the heartbeat of revival in America waits on the prayer life of God's people!

I talk to pastors regularly, and they say their number one weakness is their devotional life. The number one failure in their life is prayer. There's not a hope in the world of America returning to God if the leaders do not pray! They don't guide their churches to be preeminently houses of prayer. When Jesus said, "My house will be a house of prayer, but you've made it everything else but," He was characterizing the churches of America. Now there are some churches that have an amazing prayer life, and the impact they're having on their community is in direct relationship to their prayer life. But this is not the norm.

If we do not return to God's requirement to be His people in the midst of our nation, then the salt will not preserve, the light will not disperse darkness, and America will get worse and worse. Then God will call a halt to it. He has never allowed a nation to have the privileges we have had and squander them without judgment. I believe we're at a crossroads. We will either have revival—which is what God does to His people and then through His people—or judgment.

When I was a pastor I read the scripture in Matthew 16 in which Jesus said, "Now on this rock—that is, on the activity of My Father and the life of His children convincing people that I am the Christ, the Son of the Living God—I will build My church; and the gates of hell will not prevail against it." In light of this passage I always asked the question, Are the gates of hell coming down anywhere around our church? Is God working through us to bring down the gates of hell? If not, then we need to get back to the kind of relationship with Him in which He can; because Jesus said that wherever He plants His churches, the gates of hell *will* come down.

I talk with many, many people in the churches across America, and it doesn't seem as if they're even asking that question. But Matthew 16 is the standard that God has given. We'd better look to the standard to see if any of what God says would happen, is happening in our churches; and if it isn't happening, we must ask, "What do we need to do to adjust our lives back to God so it will?"

A century of teaching evolution as fact and decades of misinformation about the Bible have left a generation of people unsure of what to believe. Even some Christians have a weakened view of the reliability of the Bible. Grant Jeffrey wants to see the Word of God elevated back to its place of authority and honor.

Grant Jeffrey

One of the most critical issues facing the world and the church is the credibility of Christianity and the Bible. In past generations that wasn't a problem. A hundred years ago, great sinners would take an oath on the Bible without mental reservation; they knew the Bible was the Word of God, even though they didn't want to follow it themselves. Today, not only do great sinners reject the authority of the Bible, but many pastors in mainline denominations do as well! Many believers are genuine Christians but have what I would call a diminished view of biblical authority, biblical inspiration.

Where does this come from? I think it's pretty obvious that one hundred-plus years of teaching evolution as fact has produced a dichotomy, an almost double-mindedness in many Christians. If you believe that evolution is true—which it is not, but if you believe it because you've been taught it, and no one has given you contradicting information—and you become a Christian, you now have a double-mindedness. In one part of your mind, unexamined and unchallenged, you have the view that the first six chapters of the book of Genesis are absolutely false. In another part of your mind, you are trusting that other parts in that same book are absolutely true, although you can't possibly check them out—parts about heaven and hell and the like. Your very soul, your eternity, and your salvation depend on it.

Many Christians today have such a divided view, even though it is utterly contradictory. That's why, in some of my writings, I have dealt with the issue of evolution. I've been thrilled to find that evolutionists themselves are finally admitting the real reason they believe in evolution is that the alternative is creation by God, and that to them is unthinkable.

Evolution is now collapsing as a theory, but I believe that the teaching of evolution is one of the things that has brought about a weakness in the minds of many Christians when it comes to the authority of Scripture. In addition there have been the continuing attacks by the news media, by documentaries on television telling us that the Bible is full of myths, that it is archaeologically wrong, that it is scientifically invalid—all of which are false. These kinds of things are what motivated me to write *The Signature of God* and *The Handwriting of God,* two books which examine the medical, prophetic, archaeological, and scientific evidence for the Bible. The evidence in these areas absolutely establishes that the Bible is inspired—every single word.

I believe that the undermining of biblical authority is the number one issue that has led not only to people rejecting Christ and Christianity, but also to the weakness in many Christians today. As a Christian, you will never be stronger in your walk than your confidence in the authority of the Word of God. If that authority is impaired in your mind—and it has been for many Christians—then you will tend to rely on other things for your authority. You will rely on your feelings, you'll rely on your experience, you will rely on your emotions—all of which are changeable, all of which will fail.

The Word of God does not change, and that is why in past centuries most Christians were much stronger in their walk then most Christians today. The Bible was accepted absolutely. If there was one sentence in the Word of God that said something, that was enough for Martin Luther and for most Christians up until quite recently. Although Bibles are bought more than ever before, they're read less by Christians. The Word of God is not seen as being absolutely genuine, established, authoritative, and inspired, word for word. If there's one thing that I hope to accomplish in my ministry, it is to use Bible prophecy—which is such an incredible apologetic proof of the inspiration and authority of the Scripture—to elevate the Word of God back to where it used to be in the minds of Christians.

———

No matter what concerns we have for our country and our world, Max Lucado reminds us: God is still on His throne.

Max Lucado

You're almost "un-Christian" if you say, "I feel good about the way things are going." But I do. I look around and I feel a lot of hope. There are churches in our city that are stronger than they have ever been. I just left a prayer meeting for revival attended by sixty pastors and heard great reports of churches growing, good Christian schools springing up. I know there are a lot of bad things in the world, and there are a lot of difficulties that we face. But God is still on the throne, so I'm very much an optimist at heart.

What's the Secret?

All of us have concerns about our world, our nation, our church, and our lives. But there is an answer for every concern, and His name is Jesus. "Until now you have not asked for anything in my name," He said in John 16:24. "Ask and you will receive, and your joy will be complete."

Secret #10

Love Is the Very Nature of God

We who consider imitating Christ the highest honor would do well to be as loving, as helpful, and as concerned about the needs of others as we can. Even if our hearts have become cold, lonely, loveless places over the years, there is still hope for us; God can pour His living water into the sandy recesses of our hearts, and love for others can grow there again.

Before we begin this chapter, I want to share a story about something that happened to me years ago. It's not a tale of great victory but rather of great failure.

While I was going to school and working in Boston, I passed a homeless man on the street one night in the dead of winter. The man, who looked about seventy, was standing in front of a restaurant holding out a Styrofoam cup. If you know anything about Boston winters, you know they can be especially cold and brutal; yet the man stood there wearing only a scrubby, unbuttoned jeans jacket for warmth. As I approached him I could see that his eyes were glassy and his face was chapped from the wind. He looked pretty stoned, frozen, and pitiful, and as I moved closer to drop a dollar's worth of change into his cup, he began to cry out. His cries became louder and louder until they started to rattle me. I'd never been confronted with such dire need before, and I didn't know what to do. His was a cry of pain that I knew I couldn't heal, and so I was afraid—afraid to think what would become of him after I'd moved on. Instead of facing that fear, I gave him the money and continued quickly on my way. I listened to his cries growing quieter and quieter behind me until they were completely silenced by the wind.

If this were a book on creative writing, I'd ask you to take that true story and rewrite it with you standing in my shoes. What would you have done for this man? Would you have bought him a bowl of hot soup? Given him a twenty? Preached the gospel to him? What would you have done?

Steve Brown says that the problem with a lot of books today is that they are written from Sinai, where authors hidden behind ink and paper come across as having it all together. I'm here to admit that I don't have it all together. As I think back on that homeless man, I know I failed him. Not because I didn't buy him soup, give him a twenty, or preach to him, but because I didn't love him.

There are two kinds of charity. In the first kind, we write a check or drop change into a Styrofoam cup; in the second, we involve our hearts. The apostle Paul wrote, "If I gave everything I have to poor people...but didn't love others, it would be of no value whatever" (1 Corinthians 13:3 TLB). Mother Teresa, who personified compassion to our generation, once said, "Charity and love are the same—with charity you give love, so don't just give money, but reach out with your hand."

Because there are so many needs in our world today, we can easily get overwhelmed by the sheer scope of them. But let's not let that happen. Let's remember instead to pray, to love, and wherever possible, to assist those in need. Fortunately, we don't have to reinvent the wheel when it comes to helping others. Organizations such as Feed the Children, Compassion International, and World Vision already have working programs in place to get food and other basic humanitarian goods into the hands of people who most need them. I've included a list of charitable ministries that serve the poor in the appendix at the back of this book. You may want to take a look at some of these ministries. Many churches have similar programs in place on a smaller scale. Don't deny yourself an opportunity to be blessed by giving.

Christ's chief ministry on earth was to do His Father's will, and He expressed that by serving and caring for others. Love is His very nature, and because of that, it is a joy for Him to give. With prayer, persistence, and the stirring of the Holy Spirit, it can become our joy too.

Remember, our goal is not to single-handedly eradicate poverty. The Lord told us that the poor would always be with us. But when we make an effort to reach out in charity, we are agreeing with Holy Scripture and with Jesus to love and care for one another. We are living out His commandment to love others with our lives. "I tell you the truth," Jesus said, "whatever you did for one of the least of these brothers of mine, you did for me" (Matthew 25:40). The alternative, of course, is to be unloving, uncaring, and uninvolved, and how Christian is that?

I'm more drawn toward the concept of charity than almost any other aspect of my faith because it's so easy to understand. Christianity asks, "What needs to be done? What can I do? How can

I serve?" Among other things, we can sponsor and help feed a child who is hungry. We can give our extra clothing to the Salvation Army. We can get involved at church with local programs that help widows with home repairs, assist single moms with auto tune-ups, provide latchkey kids with after-school tutoring, visit men and women in prison—the list could go on and on. We can look for needs in the lives of those around us and ask the Holy Spirit to give us wisdom on how we can be utilized right where we live. When we love others, not only are we meeting their needs; we're also meeting the pressing need that each of us has to be like Jesus.

Some of us are genuinely challenged by the idea of giving away anything. If that's you, I want to encourage you to try to look at money and "stuff" the way you look at a library book. The book is yours to use, read, and cherish, but then it must go back to its rightful owner, the library. All the things you have—the car you drive, the money you spend, the home you live in, even your health—are rightfully God's. He's supplied them to you to use and enjoy. You can never really *own* anything, and neither can I. So let's ask Him what He wants us to do with these good things He's given to us. Just as the library will never run out of books, God will never run out of blessings for those who love and obey Him. They will always be there for us.

Recently I attended a charity auction. On one item the auctioneer started the bidding by saying, "Who will give me thirty dollars? Who will give me thirty dollars for this item?" No one took him up on the bid, so he lowered it. "Who will give me five dollars?" he asked. That worked! Someone said they would give five dollars; another person said ten; another, twenty; then thirty, and the bids went higher and higher. Eventually the item—which no one was willing to pay thirty dollars for at first—sold for eighty-five dollars!

What does the auction have to do with the red-hot topic of love? Plenty. When you begin to reach out in love, you don't have to put pressure on yourself to start serving at "thirty dollars." In other words, you don't have to jump into a yearlong commitment to tutor in an illiteracy program if the thought of it is overwhelming to you. But you can start serving at "five dollars." For example, you can drop off dinner to a neighbor in need, take a bag of household necessities to a homeless shelter, or sponsor a child through a humanitarian ministry like Compassion International. Don't be surprised if you find yourself one day serving at "eighty-five dollars"— not because your guilt says you're supposed to but because you want to. You just didn't know you wanted to when you started out at five!

And don't be surprised, the next time you see a homeless man or woman freezing on a street corner in the night, if the eyes of your heart see Jesus Christ standing there before you.

The gospel frees us to approach insurmountable problems with faith that a difference can be made, hope that a solution is possible, and motivation to invest ourselves in the lives of those who are less fortunate. Tony Campolo answers the question: What would you do if you had the power to change things overnight in America?

Tony Campolo

I would work very hard on creating jobs for the poor. The only way to eliminate poverty in this country—and I think that is an overriding concern for many of us—is to create jobs that people without a high level of education can fill and earn a viable salary. There are jobs for low-skilled people, but they tend to be at minimum wage without any medical benefits. I think we need to change that. Every American ought to be covered by health insurance in one way or another, and every American should be able to earn a living wage that enables him or her to support a family. You can't support a family on minimum wage.

At Eastern College where I teach, we are really committed to job creation. We have put together a graduate program that trains people to go into poor neighborhoods and start businesses in cottage industries that the indigenous people can own and run themselves. Only by owning and running their own business on the micro level will they be able to earn enough money to do the things that need to be done to keep a family intact. That's a family value, incidentally— that every family is entitled to a living wage.

I have always been committed to finding ways to reach out to people who are in need, especially the poor and the oppressed. My vision is that the last few years of my life are going to be concentrated on developing a Christian model for urban renewal that is not dependent on government funding or government subsidies but looks to the church as the primary instrument. To that end, Eastern College has gone the second mile with me. They are investing millions of dollars in developing what we call the Philadelphia Institute for Urban Studies. We're constructing the campus in the heart of the city. There, church leaders will be able to engage the city council, the mayor, and other officials, speaking on the issues of justice that concern us as Christians. We will have a training center for schoolteachers, especially teachers who are going to be in the Christian schools that are popping up all over the city. If a school voucher program is enacted at some point, there are going to be huge numbers of teachers who will need training—inner-city teachers, African-American teachers, Hispanic teachers.

We're also developing a program through the Institute to help churches start small businesses and small cottage industries for the unemployed kids that live in the neighborhood. Church buildings remain empty from Sunday to Sunday. We want to say, "Don't let this building—which is God's building—remain vacant through the week. That's bad stewardship. Each of those Sunday school rooms can house a small business, and the church office can service those businesses. The people with expertise who have retired in your congregation can serve as consultants to those businesses. Start businesses, because it's the only way to help the poor in your neighborhood long-term."

We're going to be doing urban counseling, which is very different than suburban counseling. The people who struggle with personal problems and live in the inner city have troubles that are very different from those of the rich and middle-class people living in the suburbs. At the Institute we will be formulating policy and programs that we believe, in the long run, can literally transform our cities. We feel that if we do well in Philadelphia, Christian groups in other cities will be able to replicate our model.

It's an awesome thing when members of the church dedicate themselves to their community. It's even more awesome when the desire to serve spreads through the whole church body.

Scotty Smith

As grace goes deeper into a church, mercy will be extended. There is a direct correlation between people in our church coming to know the grace of God in a deeper way and the many mercy ministries we offer—prison outreach, cross-cultural ministry, working with the poor, meeting tangible needs, feeding the hungry.

When we read the Gospels, we find that at the end of the world Jesus will come back and make His judgments this way: "I commend you for visiting me in prison. I commend you for offering me a cup of cold water. I was hungry and you fed me. I was naked and you clothed me." Understanding that Jesus will judge us based on how we help others meet the most basic needs of life has had a huge impact on this church family, and I've seen a maturing in this area.

In any big church, you typically have a part of your community—say 5 or 10 percent—that is captured by a vision of service. Perhaps you can look at that 5 or 10 percent and convince yourself that the whole church is that way. But for us, the challenge has come in asking, How do we avoid simply celebrating the 10 percent who are enjoying that kind of joyful, sacrificial lifestyle? How can the other 90 percent come to enjoy having their own hearts affected by those mercy ministries so that they do more than just look at the bulletin and say, "Look at all the ministries we have here!" We really believe that if you are called to have this church as your home, there is a towel with your name on it that's ready to wash someone's feet.

We would love to see this whole church liberated to live out the compassion, the mercy, the costly love of Jesus.

———

We can feel limited by what we have to offer others in need—especially if our concept of charity is fixed singularly on our giving money. In this story, Steve Brown talks about numerous ways to be charitable, none of which involve writing a check.

Steve Brown

One of our staff members is dying of cancer right now. He has two little children. Our staff went to his house earlier today, brought pizza, put up a Christmas tree, and played with his kids. Nobody would know that if I weren't telling you right now.

Our church is involved in ministries to homeless people and to prisoners. We often give contributions to other ministry organizations when we have the money and the need is there. We give out 350,000 free teaching tapes a year. I think these kinds of things go on among Christians wherever they are; it's not a big deal. Christians just do these things—or should.

———

Time and money are important gifts we can give, but they're not the entire picture. Our attitude is equally important because, as Paul tells us in 1 Corinthians 13, without love, our gifts do no good and our actions have no value.

Sheila Walsh

It would be hard to put into words the tremendous legacy that Mother Theresa has left behind her—the thumbprint she has left on all our souls as a life fully given over to showing Christ's love to people who have nothing. That thumbprint on my life is why I'm a board member and national spokesperson for a ministry called House of Hope, a home in Florida for teenage runaway girls. One of the lessons I've learned through working with people who give their lives to helping the poor and the homeless is that it's not enough to say, "God loves you." You need to say, "Come live with me and let me show you how God loves you." The people at House of Hope don't just go preach to the girls who are living on the streets in Florida, who are prostituting their fifteen-year-old bodies to get money for drugs. They say, "Come live with us for a year or eighteen months, and let us show you what the love of God looks like."

Some people think, "If I just write a check, my conscience will feel better and I can go on living my life." I don't think it is enough to write a check. I think you need to get involved. It is one of the things we want our son, Christian, to understand. When he was three or four, we began taking him with us to help serve in a soup kitchen. Twice a year we go through his toys, weed out the things he has not played with for a while or doesn't need, and take them to other children. I don't just get someone to come and pick them up; we take them ourselves, and Christian gives his toys to the other kids. I want him not only to appreciate what he has, but also to realize that not everyone in this world lives like he does.

Sometimes we forget that people who live in the streets are exactly like us. We rush past them; or if we stop to give some money, we are almost embarrassed to look at them. Charity without dignity is not a gift at all. That's one of the things I learned from my father before he died. He would often bring homeless people to our house, and they would join us for an evening meal. They would have a bath and get cleaned up, and suddenly I could see them as someone who could be my uncle or my aunt—not someone covered in the grime of a broken life.

If you do see someone in the street and you want to give them some money, great. But stop and talk to them for a couple of minutes. Look them in the eye and see them as a real person—not as someone you have to hurry past and give something to so you don't feel guilty.

We show compassion, caring, and love for one another when we look to meet each other's needs. Some need food or healthcare; others, housing or an education. But regardless of the physical need, each of us needs to hear the message of God's wonderful love for us.

Henry Blackaby

Love is the very nature of God. In both 1 John and the Gospel of John, God keeps saying, "You need to love one another in exactly the same way that I have loved you." If we have not grown in our understanding of His love, we will not function in love toward one another. Jesus said, "The distinguishing mark that identifies you as My disciple is the quality of the love you have one for another—not the quality of love you have for an unbelieving world but the quality of love you have for your fellow disciples." It's astounding to me how people can look at those passages in John 13, 14, 15, 16, and 17; hear what Jesus says about loving one another; and then turn right around and act in an un-Christlike way. It means either we have never known His love, or we've moved a long way away from our relationship with Him.

It is spiritually impossible for me to act in an un-Christlike way if I really have Christ living out His life in me, because His life is always expressed in a tremendous love toward others. Jesus picked up the most broken people and loved them into a whole new way of life. When the disciples said, "Keep blind Bartimaeus quiet," Jesus said, "Bring him to Me." When people wanted to stone the woman who was caught in adultery, He reached down to her and said, "I don't condemn you; just don't sin anymore." He touched lepers when the rest of the religious community would not.

How can I look at what Jesus did, touching all of the ones no one else would touch; acknowledge that He is resident in my life, seeking to live out His life in me; recognize that the Father's desire is to conform me to be like His Son—how can I look at all that and then face a broken world and not love? I would cancel everything that God has said and done. I can't do that. That's why I have a huge commitment to the broken, to the inner city, and to the Native American in particular.

I have no problem working with all racial groups and with the most broken people in poverty-stricken areas. I've been in about seventy-five countries of the world. I'm deeply committed to taking everything I know about my Lord to people wherever I go; letting them know that I'm an ordinary person, no more special to God than they are; and saying, "Let me introduce you to the one who's changed this ordinary person—and who wants to change your life."

That's my desire as we prepare right now to go to Hungary and Romania, a wonderful group of people who've missed so much of what we have taken for granted. I want to say to them, "I've come because I love you, and God loves you. Let me open the Scriptures and help you know some things about God's love for you that you can personally experience before the day is out."

Caring for another person doesn't benefit the recipient only. We who give are blessed as well. God promises to provide for us if we are generous with what He has given us.

Frank Peretti

I like the Old Testament principle of gleaning. If you grow grapes, you are commanded to leave a few grapes on the vine as you harvest them so that the poor can gather some too. If you drop some sheaves, don't go back and pick them up; leave them for the poor. If you harvest a field, leave a corner for the poor to come and glean from.

In the New Testament, Paul says to instruct the rich to be generous and ready to share their worldly wealth, because by doing so they will lay up true riches for the future. In other words, if you invest in people, give to charity, and remember to be generous, the Lord will take care of your future. He'll make sure your needs are met.

I've had a really nice relationship with the Lord in that respect. It's like we have this business arrangement going: "Frank, as long as you remain a pipeline of blessing, I'll keep sending blessing down the pipeline." So, hey, I don't throw money to the wind. I'm pretty careful about what I do with it and who I give it to. But giving is a blast; it's a lot of fun. It's very rewarding to hear about someone's genuine, sincere need and then to be able to do something about it.

———

The ability to give is a wonderful privilege. And as Max Lucado knows firsthand, we can never outgive God.

Max Lucado

Affluence is the biggest surprise of our lives. My wife, Denalyn, and I went to Brazil as missionaries, and I think our first salary was one thousand dollars a month. That wasn't great, but it was ample. It was a middle- or upper-lower-class salary in Brazil. Then I started writing books, and they started to sell, and all of the sudden we had income, real disposable income.

We try very hard to be benevolent. Denalyn has a gift of charity, so she has been aggressively benevolent. We have never, however, given sacrificially. There have been times when I thought we were going to; but just before we could give the gift, we would find out that another contract had been signed, or a book had done well, and all of a sudden we had more.

I'm absolutely convinced that if I felt the Lord calling me to give a certain amount to a church in Croatia, and I purposed to do it even though I wasn't sure where the money would come from, the money would be there by the time I wrote the check. That's happened too many times—literally a dozen times. We've enjoyed that privilege.

If we understand charity to be only a religious observance, we have missed the big picture. We must cultivate the understanding that we are to love our neighbors, love our enemies, and care for the poor. They need the resources we have to give, and we need to learn how to love others as ourselves.

Brennan Manning

Christianity is all about loving, and you can take it or leave it. If all the thousands and thousands of hours I've spent in prayer and meditation, if all the sermons I've preached, if all the books I've written do not lead to a loving heart, then my religion is bankrupt. Paul, who understood the mind of Christ perhaps better than anybody who ever lived, sums up his whole understanding of the message of Jesus in Galatians 5:6: "The only thing that matters is the faith that expresses itself in love."

According to Paul, the person who is most Christlike is not the one who spends the most time in prayer, or who has the best mastery of chapter and verse in the Bible, or who has the most Ph.D.'s, or who has the most important position of responsibility. No, the one who is most Christlike is the one who loves the most. That's not my opinion; that's the Word that will judge us in Matthew 25. "Come, you blessed of My Father, inherit the kingdom prepared for you from the creation of the world" (NKJV). Wow! I'm beloved, blessed, pleasing in the eyes of my heavenly Father to the extent that I have become a beneficiary of the kingdom of heaven. Why? Jesus says, "I was hungry, and you gave me food; thirsty, and you gave me drink; naked, and you clothed me; sick, and you comforted me; in prison, and you came to visit me."

On that day a lot us are going to protest and say, "Just a moment, sir. I never saw you in my entire life. I lived out most of my days in Nashville, Tennessee, surrounded by ordinary, dull, uninspired, and uninspiring people. How can you say I was ever kind or unkind to you when I never met you?" Then will come the revelation of revelations, the end of the greatest story ever told. Jesus will look into your eyes and mine, and say, "What you did to them, you did to Me. As often as you did it for the least of My brothers and sisters, you did it for Me."

We can't be adoring some vague deity above the clouds; we can't be worshiping Jesus in His Word and ignoring Him in those around us. Two of the central facts of Christianity are these: Christ is in you, and Christ is in me. And in the end, as Saint Augustine said, "There will be the one Christ loving Himself."

What's the Secret?

The themes covered in the gospel are so broad, so varied. But love for God and for others is central to all of them. Each one of us in the kingdom of God hears a different, individual call that leads us to our own arena of service. Let's make a commitment to serving the needy wherever we are. We may just find that in our charity, we are the ones who are most served.

In the hands of our mighty and purposeful God, history is definitely going somewhere. The future is coming, and it is a future of enjoying and serving God and one another. In the hands of our mighty and purposeful God, history is definitely going somewhere.

Secret #11

History Is Going Somewhere

I had to take two semesters of Western Civilization while I was in college. I didn't think I would like history, but then I didn't count on having Ms. Mickelson as my teacher. Ms. Mickelson had that rare and enviable ability to tell stories in such a way that she could animate dry textbooks and bring them to life. She had a knack for drama that made whatever she was teaching fascinating—whether she was talking about Copernicus and the heavenly spheres or Marie Antoinette and the French Revolution.

In just eight months we covered the Renaissance, the Reformation, and the Scientific Revolution, all the way through to the Enlightenment and beyond. Page after page of history was turned. Century after century came and went. We watched as kings fought for power, won it, then lost it and were gone. Kingdoms rose and kingdoms fell. Entire lifetimes were condensed to ten minutes of class time or less, and with every turn of the page, we passed through another era. *History is going somewhere*, we thought. *It's coming closer to us here in the twentieth century.*

Thanks in large part to Ms. Mickelson, I now think of all of history as one long story filled with a cast of millions of characters and billions of extras. It's a story that spans the millennia. But the central event of all of human history occurred two thousand years ago on a cross in Jerusalem, and it involved the crucifixion of one man. That event means more to the world than anything Galileo could discover; the appearance of the Son of God stepping into time gave back life to humanity. Now all of history waits and watches for Christ's return.

As Grant Jeffrey likes to say, "The average individual has a curiosity about the future." This chapter is dedicated to that inborn curiosity that exists in all of us. For the Christian, however, curiosity is tempered by the recognition that God possesses a plan. To God, the future isn't a mystery or a guessing game. He isn't afraid of what *might* happen. His sovereignty assures us that He does in fact have the whole world in His hands. Nothing happens outside His notice or design.

Nonetheless, He's given us free will so that we're not robots. We're able to be His children, to participate in life, and to interact with His creation. Somehow, what is paradox to our limited minds is reality in the heart of God.

In this chapter's interviews, I see each author as a surveyor, a scout, a lookout. Through their travels, each one has met up with other pastors, writers, world leaders, and missionaries who are on their own journeys. I asked the authors to report back some of what they've seen and heard. I asked questions like, "Is revival coming, or is it already here?" I asked about the health of the church, the nearness of Jesus' return, and whether God will judge our country.

I think you will find their answers intriguing, as always. They center on what God is doing in the history of our time—and how it involves us. History is definitely going somewhere. The question is, Where are you and I in the midst of it?

For Christians, interest about the future often centers on the question, Is revival coming? I asked Tony Campolo if he thought revival is on the horizon for our nation and the world.

Tony Campolo

The term *revival* intrigues me. If you mean an intense spreading of Christianity and commitment to Christ, then I would say it's not coming; I think we are already there. Everywhere I go I find people who are turning to Christ in ways they never did before. If you go out to a church like Bill Hybels's Willow Creek near Chicago and ask a simple question, "How many of you had no connection to the church at all, no commitment to Christ, before you came into the Willow Creek community?" about 80 percent out of the eighteen to twenty thousand people who show up on Sunday would raise their hands. Everywhere I go I find that people are coming into the church today who were totally outside of the church a few years ago. There is an intense awakening of Christianity in this country.

When I was a kid growing up, theological liberalism was pervasive in the church. Today it's dead; it's evaporating from the scene. Liberal churches are empty. They can't recruit new people into the ministry, and they don't recruit anybody to the mission field these days. Evangelicalism is the only form of Christianity that seems to be surviving into the twenty-first century. It has stood the test of time, and it is growing.

There's an influx of people into the household of faith like never before. If you travel around the world, you find that a tremendous gathering of souls into the kingdom of God is taking place in countries all across the globe. America may be the slowest in responding to the worldwide trend! But I believe we will catch up with the world in the twenty-first century.

———

Some Christian leaders are calling the church to become more knowledgeable about the Word of God; others are urging the body of Christ toward a more impassioned faith. Scotty Smith advocates a balanced symmetry in the hearts of believers—a church body possessing both informed minds and inflamed hearts.

Scotty Smith

I can see several things for the church of Jesus Christ, both at large and in our own community; and I can't think of one without thinking of the other. It is certainly my desire for us at Christ Community Church and my hope for American Christianity in general to see Christians brought back to that very balanced place of having informed minds and inflamed hearts. In church history, we always see the temptation to go in one of two directions: either to become cerebral and theologically oriented as the pendulum swings toward needing to be a teaching church again, or to become experience-oriented as the pendulum swings in the opposite direction toward experiencing the presence of the living God. What's been great in recent years is that the contemporary worship movement has brought men and women yet again into the profound awareness that worship is central to the whole of the biblical worldview.

a call to informed minds

Sometimes the experience of God can be dangerously disjointed from the knowledge of God. My hope for us at Christ Community is that we will always take very, very seriously the fact that God has spoken, and He has not stuttered in His Word. God has given us propositional truth. We are to have informed minds. We are to be a theologically literate people today.

It concerns me that in a lot of contemporary Christianity, we have our favorite teachers, our favorite cassettes, and our favorite books. It's almost like we have our Christian artist/author/pastor bubble gum cards. We're glad there is a Chuck Swindoll; we're glad there is a Steve Brown; we're glad there is a Chuck Colson. They're on our team. That's like having Mark McGwire on your baseball team. If you've got a few big hitters, you're glad to be playing for the team. But we're all called to get in the game.

There was a time when Charles Spurgeon, the great English pastor, was preaching in London, and the whole culture was biblically literate. You would go to get your hair cut, and your barber and your friends would be talking about the theology of Jeremiah or the implications of a prevailing philosophy as it intersects with biblical Christianity. We don't have that literacy today. We have people who know truth vicariously. We have people who hear the ring of truth but don't own it themselves. I long to see this generation of Christians become students again, but not only students: students who will realize that along with an informed mind, there should be an inflamed heart.

a call to inflamed hearts

Go back to the eighteenth century and look at New England during the Great Awakening in our own country. What was remarkable about the preaching of George Whitefield, Cotton Mather, and Jonathan Edwards was the response of the people. Christians got so excited about biblical theology and its implications that they got involved in the culture. Prisons were emptied, and orphanages were strengthened. The culture was affected, worship was deep, and the awe of God was restored.

A characteristic of worship in our culture is that we love getting to know God as Abba Father—so gentle, so close, so cuddly. But we've lost the revelation of being in awe of Him. Through the prophet Jeremiah, God warned about how lamentable it is when His people no longer have awe toward Him. How awesome would it be for you and I to live in a generation of Christians whose hearts are filled with awe of a God who loves us intentionally as He says He does? We would be students of His Word, amazed at His grace and holiness, liberated to get involved in the culture in every sphere of life for His glory.

I long to see Christians in our church and across America

becoming students, but let's not suffer dead orthodoxy for a minute. No, let's not get into the ugliness of splitting every hair and debating every nuance. Let's study the Word. Let's once again tremble at the Word of God. The whole body, from children to adults—let's be intelligent believers, but let's be impassioned believers. In the final analysis, as the bride of Christ, we are called to be both the bride faithful and the bride in love. I long for our church and this generation of believers to be the faithful bride of the Word of God as well as the bride in love, longing for the return of our bridegroom.

Indeed, history is going somewhere, and God is the one who is leading it. I asked Henry Blackaby, "Where are we going in the future?" But as he explained, that's really the wrong question.

Henry Blackaby

I had an old professor who said, "Henry, you need to ask the right questions." The question is not, Where are we going? The question is, Where is God going? A servant needs to be where his master is.

The American mind-set is that you need to have a vision for yourself. You need to set your priorities and your goals, then head toward them. Well, that's not biblical at all. A Christian has no right to set a goal. His right is to follow the Master. But many of God's people don't know how to know when God is speaking, so how in the world can they follow Him?

If you were to ask me where God is headed, I would say that God is always headed toward making sure that none perish but that every person comes to repentance. And if you were to ask me what I see God doing to that end, I would mention several things. Number one, He's opening up the countries of the world more than at any time in all of history, and number two, He's sending more missionaries. There's no question in my mind that God is right now taking the gospel to every last person on the face of the earth, and He's doing it in ways we've never seen before.

For example, I don't know when I've ever seen God move in such a lively way among teenagers. Today's youth have a commitment to see revival come to America deeper than any other generation I've seen. He is calling college students. He is calling businessmen. Never have I seen so many people entering the ministry or entering missions; never have I seen God marshal His people in this way. In our convention, more than five hundred thousand people did volunteer missions this last year. I see that same increase in other denominations, and I see it in Third World countries. Third World countries are sending more missionaries around the world than at any time in human history.

The last piece that must be in place before our Lord returns is that every people group on the face of the earth must have an opportunity to hear the gospel. That is a possibility within the next couple of years. So where are we headed in the next millennium? That's the wrong question. The question is, Where is God headed? I'm one of those who believes that we may be the generation that is alive and remains when Jesus returns. Everything I see in the Scripture points in that direction, and everything I see around me points in that direction.

I order my life based not on what I want to do for God; I order my life based on what God makes known to me He is doing.

Those are radically different bases for living. I think God is on an intense agenda to take the gospel to every people group and to pull His people back to Himself, so He can bring the kind of revival that can touch a nation and a world. I'm ordering my life in that direction.

———

One facet of the future I am most optimistic about is the passionate faith of the youth of today. Cassie Bernall became a symbol of faithfulness to Christ when she was martyred in the Columbine High School shooting in 1999. She represents the all-out dedication to Christ that her generation demonstrates in their intensity of worship and service.

Frank Peretti

I'm optimistic about the future. We Christians still have our bouts with being childish about things, but what encourages me is the young generation coming up. There are some fantastic revivals going on among teenagers and young people. I've read about and met some of these youth, and they are truly the church of the future. They're strong, dedicated saints. I'm really encouraged to see them.

You read about all the problems going on in the world, and it's true. There's a lot of wickedness in the world, and our country is in some of the throes of that. But at the same time, there might just be a turnaround happening. You see, there's a great increase in church attendance. The children of the baby boomers are now having families of their own, and they are feeling the need to return to their religious roots and reestablish some kind of a foundation for themselves and their children.

Everybody is quite aware that there's something wrong, that we've got a real moral crisis. We've got to get back to the basic moral foundations, not just as a nation, but as families, as individuals. Everybody knows that God has got to fit into the equation somewhere, and that God is the answer to the dilemma that we're in. People know that we've got to return to the Lord, we've got to get back to where we were, we've got to get our act together and get right with God. We've had our ups and downs. Things have been bad before. But we've had revivals, too, and resurgences of religion and morality. Right now, I'm encouraged. I don't know that the world is going to get any better, but I've got very high hopes for God's people.

———

The church is changing. Denominational walls are coming down, and church people are becoming more and more open about their moral and spiritual problems. As Max Lucado explains, these are very healthy signs.

Max Lucado

I see two things happening in the church today. One is that denominational walls are becoming very frail; they're all but down. That's a very healthy sign, because that's a precursor to revival. Whenever there's unity, there's the opportunity for coordinated prayer, which then can spur revival.

Secondly, there is a rawness to the kinds of problems church people have. When I say rawness, I mean Internet pornography, adultery, drug addiction. The churches are full of people who are dealing with these issues. I'm not sure if all churches are prepared and open to help these people. That's not a new problem; but I think people's willingness to be open about these problems is pretty new, and that's encouraging.

———

What is God doing right now that will have an impact in the future? According to Steve Brown, God is calling us to become more like Christ.

Steve Brown

I feel excited about the church as we move into the new millennium because I really believe God is trying to call us back to be more like Christ. I see that happening in a lot of places. Our culture is forcing us to that, and I think it is a good thing.

At the same time, there are a lot of issues that worry me. I read all the books bemoaning the evangelical morass we are in—how we're not faithful to the Bible or theology or whatever somebody's agenda is. The trouble with those books is that they are always spoken from Sinai. I would read books like that if the first chapter were a confessional chapter. Then I could understand the rest of the chapters. The great danger is that we have become religious; we speak from Sinai and no longer see the power of God operating in our lives. We engage in a lot of critique of other Christians that is very arrogant, and I think sometimes we need to be broken. When we're not broken, we are very religious and very insightful and very profound and very dead.

———————

People have always been curious about the future, and as Grant Jeffrey knows, there is a renewed interest in biblical prophecy today. Grant explains the cyclical appeal of prophecy over the last two millennia.

Grant Jeffrey

Throughout history and especially in the last two hundred to three hundred years, as the church reacquired what I call a literal hermeneutic, a literal method of interpreting prophecy and other passages of the Bible, it was natural for prophecy to become understandable. This was how the early church understood prophecy in the first two hundred years; they interpreted the prophecies in a literal, futurist way. In fact, in one of my books, *Apocalypse*, I show how eighty-five major details of prophecy that people like Hal Lindsey, Jack Van Impe, and myself teach as literal—such as a rebuilt temple, a return to animal sacrifices, an actual Antichrist man, a literal mark of the beast—were also taught as literal in the first three centuries, indicating that the early church understood prophecy more or less as we do.

You have to understand that the Bible was out of the hands of the average person for almost one thousand years through the Dark Ages. Therefore, there was little study of any parts of the Bible, let alone prophecy. Many priests could not read. But when the Bible became available after the Protestant Reformation, it was read by the average Christian. It was natural that interest in prophecy arose, since one-quarter of the Bible is prophetic.

During the last three hundred years, there have been what I would call *waves* of interest in prophecy; you find twenty-five to fifty-year spans over which a lot of people were reading and writing about Bible prophecy. But when Christ did not come as the people expected, those waves ran out, and there would be a trough of relatively small interest for another period of thirty years or so. Then it would rise again.

In 1970 Hal Lindsey wrote *The Late Great Planet Earth*, and that was really a milestone in terms of creating the wave of interest in eschatology that we are now in. He did what no one thought could be done: He took prophecy out of the libraries of pastors and brought it to the interest level of the average Christian and even non-Christian. He dealt with prophecy in a way that anyone could understand, whether they were Jesus people or people who had no interest in the Bible whatsoever. He made prophecy popular, and he was criticized for this. But what he knew—and I have often talked about this—is that prophecy is valuable as an apologetics and evangelism tool, since the average individual has a curiosity about the future. That's why you see horoscopes in every newspaper in the country. That's why there are psychic hot lines. There's an inborn curiosity about our future in every man and woman.

God commands us to teach the whole counsel of God. Since prophecy is 25 percent of the Bible, we must teach those truths about the Second Coming. We must teach those truths about the reality of heaven and hell. Tragically, many pastors have admitted to me that fewer than two hours out of the three or four years they spent in seminary dealt with heaven, the resurrection body, the Second Coming. These subjects were glossed over. Yet they've been a dominant topic in the church's teaching and the church's singing over the centuries. John and Charles Wesley wrote five thousand hymns, and the vast majority were on the Second Coming and the reality of heaven. We need to get back to the biblically based realities that the Second Coming is the focus toward which we are heading as a church, and the establishment of Jesus Christ's kingdom on earth is the goal of history as defined by the Word of God.

———◆———

The old adage says that there are two certainties in life: death and taxes. Most people are frightened about the subject of death—but Christians don't have to be. As we get older, heaven becomes more real to us because of the people who have gone before us, and interest in our earthly life wanes.

Barbara Johnson

I'm living somewhere between estrogen and death, OK? I have deposits in heaven, and as I get older, I have more and more deposits there. There's a verse in Psalm 90:10 that says, "The years of our lives are three score and ten. Soon they are gone and we will fly away." That's what I believe. Either He's going to come back for me, or by death I'm going to go to Him.

It's exciting to think of what heaven contains because I have deposits there. This world has nothing that is of any entertaining value to me. When people say, "Name it and claim it," I say, "I don't want it!" There's nothing here that's holding me. I think we're just pilgrims here; we're not settlers. Hang on loosely to your job, to your children, to your home, and to your possessions, because all of this is going to fade. Only what's eternal really counts.

I heard a story recently about a lady who was going to die, so she called her pastor over to plan the funeral service. She told the pastor, "I want to have a fork in my hand so that people will go by my casket and see the fork." He said, "Well, why in the world would you want that?" And she answered, "Whenever I go to a wonderful banquet and the servers begin to clear away the dinner plates, someone always says, 'Now hold on to your fork.' That means something wonderful is coming, like a fancy desert or a wonderful soufflé. So when people go by my casket and they see the fork, they'll ask you why it's there. And you can say, 'Because the best is yet to come.'"

See, heaven is going to be so wonderful for us. Death doesn't hold any pain for me because I don't think we ever say good-bye for the last time. Christians never say good-bye for the last time. I think death is God's way of saying, "Your table is ready." Death is not extinguishing the light; it's just turning down the lamp because the dawn has come. I'm not afraid of death. I mean, I'm ready to go whenever the Lord takes me.

In my book *He's Gonna Toot and I'm Gonna Scoot*, I write many things to encourage people who have been through or are going through a very difficult time facing the imminence of death. People really need encouragement. Recently, I got a note from a man, along with a check for the price of some of my books. A week earlier, his wife had been at one of our conferences. I always tell the girls at my book table, "If somebody comes up and doesn't have the money or doesn't have a check, just give them the books; that's OK." That's probably why we get rid of them so quickly—we give them away!

This woman had been given some books, and now her husband was paying for them. His note was not very nice. It said: "Do not send me your newsletter. Do not send me anything. Do not sell my name to anybody!" I decided I would call him up since his telephone number was on the check. I called and said, "This is Barbara Johnson." The name didn't mean anything to him. I said, "I just got your check today, and I was wondering what you were doing at the women's conference."

At first he sounded really bitter. He said, "Well, it was my wife who wanted the books, and they gave them to her. So when she came home from the meeting, she told me to make out a check to some lady to pay for them." He continued, "I knew it would mean more people asking me for money, more people wanting to put me on their mailing list, more people sending me their newsletters—"

I interrupted and said, "Look, I've got two big boxes of names of people who want to get my newsletter, and I can't even put them on! We don't put people on mailing lists. We don't sell your name." And the more I talked to him, the more I could see that he was really hurting.

"My wife has cancer," he said, "and they told her at Christmas she only has three months to live. I didn't want her to go to that women's thing, but she wanted to go. They picked her up in her wheelchair. But she didn't have any money in her purse, and so they gave her these books at your book table."

We talked a little bit more, and then he said, "Would you like to talk to my wife?" I said, "Oh, I'd love to talk to her." So he gave her the phone and left the room—somewhat embarrassed, I think—and I talked to her. She said, "You know, at the meeting you talked about a book you just wrote called *He's Gonna Toot and I'm Gonna Scoot*, and I would just love to read it. But I'll be gone by the time it comes out." This was January, and the book wasn't due out until April. I said, "Well, I have a manuscript of the book. It's all scribbled over, but I'd be glad to send it overnight to you—not to him, but to you. I think it will help you."

So I sent the book, and a couple of days later the woman called. She said, "I read the book, and it was a balm for my soul. It was so wonderful." Then she said, "I have a favor to ask. Would you do something for me?" I said, "Oh honey, I'd do anything for you." And she said, "Well, when I'm gone my husband is going to be so desolate and so alone. Would you put him on the list to get your newsletter every month?" I got such a kick out of that because his attitude obviously had softened and changed, and so had mine. As we get to know people's hearts, as we begin to see what's inside and find out about the pain they're going through, we react so much better to them!

For Christians, the future is ultimately in heaven with the Lord. We started this chapter with Tony Campolo, and it seems appropriate to end the chapter with Tony's answer to the question, "What is heaven going to be like?"

Tony Campolo

I haven't got a clue! Someone once said, "I know nothing about the temperature of hell nor the furniture of heaven, but I believe in both." I would hold to that. I've always liked that old Chinese saying, "One world at a time, please." That is very much where I am. I have no concept of heaven, primarily because I'm sure it's such a totally other-existence that it is beyond any kind of description whatsoever. I do know this: The relational aspects of being with Jesus and being with the people of God in intensive fellowship are sufficient to make it glorious.

The kingdom of God is another story. When we pray the Lord's Prayer, we pray, "Thy kingdom come, Thy will be done on earth." We evangelicals have a tendency to ignore that phrase. We often posit the kingdom of God in another world. But the kingdom of God is something that we are supposed to see happen on earth! That's why we must be committed to social justice, to changing the world into the kind of world that God wants it to be—knowing all the while that we can never complete the task. That's what the Second Coming is all about. "The good work that He begins in us," says the apostle Paul, "He will complete in the day of His coming."

We are to be a kingdom people working for justice, trying to eliminate poverty, transforming social institutions like the family into what they ought to be, and winning people to Christ, which is the most important thing. We do these things with the assurance that the good work that we have begun—that the Holy Spirit has initiated in us—will be brought to fruition, completeness, and ful-fillment when the Second Coming of Christ occurs.

What's the Secret?

In the hands of our mighty and purposeful God, history is definitely going somewhere. The future is coming, and Jesus is returning soon. Let's get ready by committing our lives today to serving God and one another.

*Church, as Max Lucado put it so well, is a home for
heart. Each of us needs to find our place in God's house
prayer—and who want
the Church, as Max Lucado put it so well, is a home for
heart. Each of us needs to find our place in God's house of*

Secret #12

Church Is a Home
for Every Heart

I'd have to say my earliest experiences of going to church were pretty grim. When I was a child, our Sunday school class met in a small, dimly lit room in the basement of the church where sour-faced teachers disciplined and drilled us. What a nightmare! What should have been a wonderful opportunity to be exposed to the gospel through patience, teaching, and the example of godly men and women was actually a gloomy exercise in rote memorization—turning the house of God into a house of frowns. Was that really what church is supposed to be? Let's hope not!

Today I love being in church because I understand better the integral parts of church life, and they've become irreplaceable to me. Church is where we hear a message proclaimed by the pastor, taught and explained from the pages of the Bible. His insights, prayerfully presented each week, are thought-provoking and Spirit-filled. Church is where we praise God through music, joining together as a band of worshipers. It's the place where we contribute our tithes and offerings, uniting our resources so that the church can remain strong and healthy and the work of ministry can continue vigorously. It's where we pray together as a family, agreeing in the sight of God that we are open and willing to be changed by His Spirit. And church is where we come together as individuals to strengthen and encourage one another to grow more like Jesus in our hearts, attitudes, and actions.

Church is made up of people—men and women with individual talents, skills, and gifts. As Christians, we offer back our gifts to Him to be used in His work. Whether we're especially gifted at music, service, administration, teaching, working with children, or encouraging others, we bring our abilities to church and share them, like friends bringing different necessary items to a picnic (barbecue, iced tea, paper plates, pie!) The church is all about family, love, being together, and above all, serving one another like Christ to meet the critical needs we can't take care of on our own (and aren't supposed to in the first place).

The church is Christ's body. Jesus is our leader and our example of how we ought to relate to one another. If we were good enough without Christ's example, no teaching on behavior would be needed. But the truth is, we're not good enough. A teacher is absolutely essential.

The Holy Bible, through the teachings of Jesus and the inspired words of the apostles, gives us a blueprint for building relationships with one another. And the church is the community in which much of the building takes place. The Spirit of God in others helps to shape us to be more like Christ—and His Spirit in us helps to shape the people around us.

In this chapter I asked the authors to share their views of the church—what it is and what it can be. Is it possible that church life can give us a foretaste of heaven? Can we be honest in church about our shortcomings and those sins that challenge us? If we all believe in Jesus, why do we disagree on particular aspects of doctrine and practice? As each of the authors attests, there is a myriad of blessings to be found within the context of church life! But these blessings remain theoretical until we step inside the doors and join the community of faith.

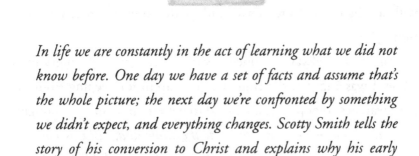

In life we are constantly in the act of learning what we did not know before. One day we have a set of facts and assume that's the whole picture; the next day we're confronted by something we didn't expect, and everything changes. Scotty Smith tells the story of his conversion to Christ and explains why his early church environment wasn't sufficient in itself to lead him to the Savior.

Scotty Smith

I grew up in the central part of North Carolina, in the Bible Belt. My family always went to church, but it was what I would call a "neo-orthodox" church. That may be a little too sophisticated; just call it "Southern cultural religion." It was not liberal, and it was not conservative. I was raised in a culture that basically thought that everybody is born a Christian, and you are a Christian until you choose not to be one. In our home, the things of God were more assumed than spoken. We never prayed as a family. We never had family devotions. I was raised knowing that God—whoever He was—was important. But my faith was far more superstitious and cultural than it was grounded in any way, shape, or form in Scripture or personal relationship.

The night I became a Christian, I was kind of surprised. To that point I had never thought about *becoming* a Christian; I thought I was one! But I had to realize that I wasn't what I thought I was. I had to realize what it actually means to become a Christian—to have a personal relationship with Christ, to be born into the family of God through a faith relationship and not simply through a relationship with a religious culture. That kind of thinking was pretty revolutionary!

Since I had always assumed I was a Christian, I was angry for a while. I was angry at the church I grew up in for keeping from me any awareness that people are called to believe something. I thought, *Why didn't anyone ever tell me that the Bible said, "But as many as received Him, to these He gave the right to become children of God"?* Why was it assumed that I just believed these things because I went to church all my life? That's like saying if a cat has her kittens in an oven, they must be cookies!

> *Scotty went on to become a pastor. But while a pastor's calling is to be celebrated and respected, Scotty believes that all ministries, gifts, and callings are to be honored. When each of us is doing what we're called to, the church becomes a symphony of praise to God.*

I can find no verse in all of Scripture that says pastors are to live a mono-dimensional life and simply walk around as clerics. First and foremost, a pastor is a member of the body of Christ who has particular gifts and callings, just as any other member of the body of Christ has certain gifts and callings. As I read 1 Corinthians 12, Paul paints a beautiful picture of God giving his church various ministries, callings, and gifts. They're all to be celebrated; they're all to be valued.

We have a natural temptation to exalt certain gifts over other gifts. But Paul makes it clear that God's paradigm is upside-down from ours. He calls the little things large and the large things small. And so, as I ponder my calling as a pastor, I see myself showing up here at church, bringing my gifts to bear upon the body, assuming that every other believer is bringing their gifts to bear. And the combination of all the gifts together, under the influence of God's Spirit and in the interest of the gospel, becomes a symphony of worship and praise to God.

I think really my calling as a pastor is to do what I do to the glory of God, in the same way a lawyer, or a guitar stringer, or anyone else is called to do his or her work to the glory of God. This compartmentalized notion of a pastor as a religious figure who walks into the room and people stop telling dirty jokes or they sit up or they get religious or they try to say something spiritual—that insults me. It offends me that people have the idea that pastors are some kind of antiseptic antibodies floating around in the culture! That's just so wrong.

It has been freeing for me to realize that a pastor is primarily called to live out his or her love relationship with the living God in the midst of the culture and the people of God and invite everyone else to join in. We are leaders. We lead best not by being religious but by being people who are astonished at the gospel and willing to be vulnerable and transparent about our own brokenness, longings, fears, pains, and sin. Then we lead the brigade to the river of grace.

The pastors who have impacted my life are not those who have been homiletic geniuses or who have had the keenest oratorical skills; they are those who have wrestled with the question, What does it mean to lay hold of the only love that will not let me go? That's the kind of pastor I want to be.

———————◆———————

The church is like a hospital, a place where we come to heal. But healing requires us to admit that we are sick in the first place. Confession is that act where we admit our impatience, our lust, our greed, and our sin. Some people ask, "Can we really confess our faults and our failures to one another? What would the church be like if everyone did that?" Max Lucado has the answer.

Max Lucado

When people share openly about their struggles, the church is being the church. God doesn't work in the darkness. It's a spiritual truth that until things are out in the light, He can't change us. But if we confess our sins, He is faithful and just to forgive our sins. We have to get things out into the light! I believe the church is God's "safe place" to make risky decisions. If the church can be less and less a place where you come to be perfect and more and more a place where you come to be healed—less and less a country club and more and more a hospital—then I think we're heading in the right direction.

I'm under the conviction that for every pain in a given congregation, there is a person in that congregation who can help ease that pain if we can just get those two people together. The problem is, we preachers get in the way. We think we have to fix everything. But it's the Holy Spirit's church, and He'll teach us how to get out of the way.

I like the thought that the church is a home for every heart. Church is a home, a place where people can find protection and safety. Jesus says, "My desire is that My house be a house of prayer for all people; a house where no person is turned away, where the doors are wide open." It's a home for the heart. The heart is that place where God does the work in the soul of man. Yes, we feed and clothe the bodies of the people we touch; but we're in the heart-changing business most of all.

———

The church is about caring—caring for the lonely, for the broken, for the ill, for the lost. As Barbara Johnson knows, the church is you and me searching compassionately for those who are forgotten and reaching toward them with the love of Christ.

Barbara Johnson

At Spatula Ministries we keep a record of all the people who have lost a child during the year. We keep the first name of the child, when he or she died, and the family's telephone number. Then starting on the first of December I begin to call every family, saying, "This is the first year without your child (use the child's name), and

I know it is going to be a hard Christmas. I just want you to know we're thinking about you, and we haven't forgotten you."

Some of these families are so alone; they haven't even told anyone why their child died. Their house is dark. They haven't decorated for Christmas. Nobody mentions the child's name. It's a lonely time for them. To have someone call from California and say, "I remember your son, and I know what you are going through"—that means a lot.

Our phone bill at that time of year is around five thousand dollars, but we call everybody on the list, even if we're still calling right up to Christmas or beyond. Then the boomerang comes, because in January I start getting letters from the people I called, saying, "We were thinking it would be a terrible Christmas. But you called us and showed us that somebody remembered our boy, and he wasn't forgotten." Hearing that is such a joy to me!

———◆———

Steve Brown made his most serious commitment to Christ while he was already pastoring a church in Boston, Massachusetts. There he committed himself to the Lord and started to earnestly teach the Bible. The congregation began to grow, and what had been a dying church was brought back from the brink.

Steve Brown

It was very interesting in those early days after I committed my life to the Lord. I didn't know what the Bible said, but I knew that people always told new Christians to start in John. So I opened the Bible in the pulpit at this very stately Presbyterian church in the city of presidents, read a verse, and explained what it meant. I stayed about one verse ahead of the congregation, and God brought revival!

The church had been dying. The Boston newspapers had done major stories on its problems. Everybody expected the church to die—and then it started growing. Our Sunday school doubled and then quadrupled. We started a Sunday evening service, and people couldn't even get into the parking lot. Honestly, all I was doing was reading a verse and explaining it. I got to the sixth chapter of John and said, "Lord, I know You told me to do this. But I've told the people everything I know, and You keep repeating Yourself!"

I didn't even know about missions at that point. I called a man named Sam Moffitt in Korea and said, "Somebody told me that you love Jesus and believe the Bible, and if you do, I will send you some money. Not only that, if you can give me the name of other missionaries who love Jesus and believe the Bible, I will send them money too." There was dead silence on the other end of the line. Finally Sam said, "Well, yeah…I can work on that." We set up a missions conference, and I didn't even know what a missions conference was!

Most believers want to be a part of a church that's growing, positive, and alive. I asked Steve to tell me what he thought the difference was between a living church and a dying church, since he had experienced both. I asked, "What was it that turned your dying church into a living one?"

The answer is simple: Jesus. I mean, He really was the reason. You remember in Scripture where Jesus was accused of planning to destroy the temple? Of course the charge was false; He was talking about His body. But there is a sense in which that charge is true.

When Jesus leaves the building, when Jesus leaves the church, you can keep it running if you have a lot of money and a lot of organization. But in terms of the lifeblood of what the church is all about, when Jesus is present, lives get changed; when He's not, we do religion. That sounds awfully pietistic, but I believe that's the difference between a living church and a dying church.

growing through grace

I don't know how familiar you are with our Key Life ministry, but it is a ministry of grace. We tell God's people that He is not angry with them. We explain that if you don't do it right, if it isn't real to you, Jesus won't stop loving you. Grace is the major principle of individual growth and church growth.

When I learned this message of grace and began to teach it, I discovered that it can make people very angry. I was speaking at a conference in Virginia, and some people got angry. I knelt down and said, "God, I'm not doing this anymore. You gave me this platform, but I think I am messing up Your people, and You know I don't want to do that! I think I am the only one speaking this message. You've got to give me a sign. I'm not doing this anymore until I know it is from You."

The next morning at the conference, a guy came up after I had spoken and said, "Steve, I like your teaching." I thought it was one of those passing, "nice sermon, pastor" comments, and I said, "Thank you." But he didn't leave. He smiled and said, "I've heard it before."

"What do you mean?" I said.

And he answered, "Jack Miller has been teaching that message for years." He didn't understand the tears that welled up in my eyes at that moment. His comments were the answer to my prayer the night before!

So I called Jack Miller. I talked to him often on the phone, and his teaching came to mean more to me than I can tell you. When he died it was a great loss to the church. I miss him a lot because his was a voice of great intellectual depth and profundity that spoke the message of grace without compromise.

the dance of freedom

Living a life of grace is like dancing without looking at your feet. A lot of us think that if we just look at our feet and learn to dance right, then the world will want to dance with us. But they are attracted more to the joy of the dance than to how we dance. People are always saying, "If you are not a good person, you will hurt your witness." I've never met anybody who was led to Christ by my goodness! I've seen them led to Christ by the fact that I'm forgiven; there is great joy in knowing you're forgiven!

I don't want anybody to think that I don't believe that purity is important or that we're called to be a holy people. We just go about purity and holiness the wrong way. Jack Miller used to say, "All of theology can be summed up in two sentences: Cheer up, you're a lot worse than you think you are." Then he would smile and say, "But cheer up, God's grace is a lot bigger than you think it is." We should be living our lives with that recognition, and that creates in us not only joy but love. We no longer have the need to be right or the need to pretend we're good. We've become beggars telling other beggars where we've found bread. And when people say, "You're not a very good person," we don't have to defend ourselves and say, "Yes, I am."

That's freedom. That's what the life of grace is, and I think it's attractive to other people.

There is great joy because you don't have to look at your feet when you dance. There is humility without being a weenie—a recognition that God was doing fine before you came along, and long after you're gone, He will do fine. There is a sense of wonder and amazement that His love has been poured out for you.

Some perceive church as a place for "good people"—those who don't mess up or make mistakes. They think they need to get their act together before they will be welcomed in church. But that just isn't true. God welcomes each of us to begin following Him just as we are.

Chonda Pierce

I grew up in a denomination where you get saved, then you get sanctified, and then you're done. But somewhere along the way you'd mess up, and you'd think you must not have been saved. It was a constant two steps forward and four steps back. You finally get to the point where you give up and cry, "I just can't do this!" Or someone finally explains the gospel to you in such a way that you think, *Oh, OK. I'm still saved. I messed up, but God still loves me.*

As a comedian I have this standard line: "I grew up and got saved 365 times and my husband got saved once, and that ticks me off!" Somewhere it got explained to him a little differently, and he got it first time off the bat. Of course, he used to think you don't have to grow anymore after you get saved. That's not so either. As long as we're in this world, we're taking steps toward our perfection. Once in a while we get a step ahead; we have a good day. I don't know; I may be wrong. When we get to heaven, everybody can point their fingers at me and say, "Aha! You were supposed to be perfect."

———

When we least expect it, we can lose our footing and tumble. Fortunately, the church is made up of people who pick us up, dust us off, and set us back where we belong.

Patsy Clairmont

We've had some pretty funny things happen on the platform at the Women of Faith conferences. At one conference, stools were set up on the stage in a small circle, and the speakers were called one by one out of the audience and up onto the platform to sit on a stool. We faced the audience with our backs to each other. We figured this would work well in the circular arena.

The only problem is I'm five feet tall, and having my little heels on doesn't help a lot. I hadn't seen this as a problem. I made it up to the platform with the rest. We sat down on the stools just as we were supposed to. Then one by one we took the microphone, stood up, walked away from our stool, gave a little introduction, handed the mike off to the next woman, and sat back down.

When my turn came, I got off the stool fine and did my presentation all right. I moved back and handed the mike to Sheila Walsh. But when I went to sit down, I didn't make it to the top of the stool. The stool and I started for the stage. Two of the gals caught me just before I splattered myself across the platform. Sheila was talking and trying not to notice that a quarter of an inch from her elbow, I had just made a downward thrust with my whole being. The girls helped me up, steadied the stool, and made sure that I got all the way onto the seat this time. Then we went on as if nothing had happened! As I told the group later, the wonderful thing about denial is that we can disconnect and pretend that I did not just fall in front of fifteen thousand people!

That incident is a picture of what living in the body of Christ is all about. There are going to be times when people think they know what they're doing, but they haven't measured things well. They're going to fall. How wonderful that these women were right there willing to grab hold! Rather than saying, "That's her problem; let her figure it out," they immediately reached for me, steadied me, and helped me to get back to the place I needed to be. And isn't that Scripture?

As believers, each of us is a part of the body of Christ. We con-nect with one another because we have the same Spirit from God. We're all individuals, yet we're attached; we're unique, yet we're imbued with so much in common. I asked Patsy to talk about the paradox.

I love that about God—He put both ingredients inside of us. We have great similarity while maintaining absolute individuality. Only God could put those two things into one being! We may seem different from one another in a lot of respects; but I'll say something in a conference, and I'll see other women nod. They've felt the same thing, but they have never articulated it, or they didn't know that it was all right to say it out loud. Suddenly it makes sense to them.

When I'm in large arenas with Women of Faith, people ask me, "What's bringing the women in?" And I say it is absolutely a movement of the Lord on the hearts of women. There is nothing in an arena that would draw a woman. I mean, arenas were built by men for men, for the purpose of sports and spitting. There's no lace on the chairs; none of the seats are pink. There's nothing that would naturally draw a woman there. Yet I watch women of all ages climb up a gazillion steps to get to their seats next to the ceiling so they can peer down on a stage. I say to myself, *This is so unnatural except for God!*

I think women are drawn to the opportunity to connect with one another. They watch me and the other team members connecting with each other on the platform. Repeatedly they come up and say, "I want to have friends like you have friends. I want to have what I see you demonstrating on that platform as you interact with one another's lives." I've stood back and asked myself, *What is it that they're seeing?* One thing they see, I think, is that we enter into each other's successes; we are able to celebrate them rather than be intimidated by them. It is a human tendency, when we see someone else doing well, to feel like we have to process that success through our own value. We ask, "What does their success mean about my value?" rather than entering in and saying, "Look what God has done in this life! Look how He has uniquely designed this person to be capable of speaking or singing or playing an instrument or interacting with people or whatever and to do it so well!" We need to have the interior freedom and the security of knowing who we are in Christ to be able to enter into another person's successes like that.

We've all heard people say, "I don't go to church; I feel closer to God just walking on the beach." But as Brennan Manning suggests, each of us needs to be part of a faith community.

Brennan Manning

Echoing John Donne's "No Man Is an Island," we are each a part of the continent, a piece of the main; and it is virtually impossible to live a life of authentic discipleship without a support group, large or small. I don't personally know of anybody who has ever succeeded in following Jesus without mentors or, as we call them in the Catholic tradition, spiritual directors. I don't know of anybody who has succeeded over a period of time without a faith community of some kind to lend encouragement, to challenge, and to reinforce. As God said in the Book of Genesis, it is not good for man to be alone. The degree of community can vary from person to person; but regardless of your extroversion or introversion, a supporting group is indispensable.

Dietrich Bonhoeffer said, "Friendship is by far life's rarest and most precious treasure and must constantly be defended against the disapproving frowns of moralism." I echo Bonhoeffer: Friendship is life's rarest and most priceless treasure. My friendship with Jesus has been without any reservation or hesitation the greatest thing that's ever happened in my life—and through Him, a handful of friendships have been priceless.

living in community

My time as a priest with the Little Brothers of Jesus was the easiest chapter of my life in a sense. It was a life of hard manual labor, but it was stress-free. I had my job as the *aguador*, or water carrier, in a little village in Spain. In the mornings I would feed the donkey and then hitch up the little buckboard. I'd go out about a mile and a half into the semiarid desert to the place where the water was kept, singing to myself the whole way. My container held six hundred gallons. So six hundred times I would dip into the water with a bucket and fill up the container. Then I'd put a cap on the container, turn around, and go a mile and a half back into town.

A customer would order water since there was no running water in the village. Everyone had a pool in the backyard. It wasn't like a swimming pool in America; it was just a great, big hole in the ground covered with cement. I would dump the six hundred gallons of water into the cement hole, and the customer would pay me about twenty cents. That was the water the family would use for bathing and cooking but not for drinking. There was—just as we have here—a special kind of water for drinking. Then I'd turn around and head back to the *arriba* to fill up my buckboard again with more water for another customer.

It was a pressure-free life, very leisurely and slow-paced. They say that if you live in a Spanish village for a year, your heart rate will slow ten beats! All in all, it was a wonderful opportunity to experience God in nature and in the people to whom I brought water.

brotherly love

A sense of fraternal love flourished on a community level in the Little Brothers of Jesus that I've never experienced before or since. The community was comprised of the same kind of folks you have in any community. We had young, middle-aged, old; we had conservatives, liberals. But because of our fidelity to three hours of prayer every day, love was very evident. I mean, you couldn't go to bed at night if you hurt somebody. On the way up the stairs, you'd kneel down and ask for forgiveness!

We did a little exercise every week called "the review of life." The six of us in the group would sit in a circle, and somebody would lead a prayer. Then we would discuss three things: first, what we learned in prayer that week; second, our successes or failures at work (we were all doing manual labor of some kind); and third, our fraternal relations. The first night we were going to do this, I thought, *This will be a very lightweight experience. All right, guys, love you all—it's been a great week!*

But it didn't work that way. In our group we had a Frenchman, a German, a Korean, a Spaniard, an Englishman, and myself. That first night the little Frenchman, whose name was Christian, came and knelt down beside my chair. I wondered, *What's going on here?* And he began, "Brennan, you're the only American in the group, and we all know how you suffer with the cold."

You see, we lived in an unheated, two-story stone house in the forest of Bregonia, where the temperature would get down to ten or twenty degrees. The only heat in the house came from a pot-bellied stove in the kitchen. At night the bedrooms upstairs were really cold. Christian said, "I know how you suffer with the cold, but we laugh at you because you have nine blankets on your bed."

He continued, "What nobody knows is that I suffer with the cold, too, and I also have nine blankets on my bed. Last night I found an extra blanket in the cupboard, and instead of putting it on your bed, I put it on mine." His eyes filled with tears. "I have not treated you as my little brother. I've been very selfish. Would you please forgive me?"

His words went through me like a dagger. The guy found an extra blanket, he put it on his own bed, and now he was in tears asking me to forgive him!

That kind of thing happened every day. The sun was never allowed to set on our anger. There are always the inevitable conflicts and tensions when a group of men live together in a community; that's unavoidable. You're not supposed to be shocked or horrified when a conflict or a misunderstanding occurs. The important thing is what you do with it after it happens. I was so deeply moved by the Frenchman's apology. I was so edified, not just by his willingness, but by his *eagerness* to seek reconciliation before going to bed that night. That was a rich experience.

———

In his book The Visitation, *Frank Peretti takes a sobering look at large, impersonal megachurches through his character, Travis Jordan. Since Frank created Travis, I wanted to know how closely his concerns about church life matched his character's.*

Frank Peretti

The size of a church isn't really the issue; the issue is the personality of the church. There are big churches that manage to retain the human element, where people and touching lives on an individual basis is important. They still run into a logistical nightmare: What are we going to do with all these people? Where are we going to seat them? Where are they going to park? How are we going to handle the traffic? How are we going to keep track of everyone? That's a problem. But members still feel like they're important, like somebody cares about them. They have a connection with people in the congregation. They have friends. They have direct support.

There are other churches, however, that are really huge, and it's as if the institutions themselves and their leadership style have become predominant. I suppose the organization can become so polished, so powerful, and so rich that people become secondary to the organization. It's the program that counts. Running things smoothly. Herding the masses in and out. It's the TV cameras.

The large church experience that Travis had in *The Visitation* is based on a large church experience I had. This was a case in which the church—the leadership style, the organization, somewhere, somehow—became so big and so polished and so organized that it was like a big bulldozer that would run you over rather than gently pick you up and nurture you. It was a powerful ministry; it was successful. Obviously, there were people of the big-city mentality, I suppose, who didn't mind being anonymous, unknown, unneeded. Perhaps they enjoyed being able to simply drop into a church and drop out again without being known or cared about.

But my wife, Barbara, and I came from a small church background where you were always needed. The church always needed help with something, whether it was teaching Sunday school or chaperoning the youth or just passing out the bulletins to people coming in the front door. They always needed you for something, and you could always be a part. At the big church we attended, you couldn't be a part. You were expected to come in, be part of the crowd, put your offering in the plate, and leave—but don't ask to be involved, don't ask to help, and don't expect anyone to remember your name! It was an illustration to me of how you can have "ministry" but leave people totally out of it.

Have you ever wondered why so many people who genuinely love Jesus still disagree on various doctrines of the Christian faith? I asked Tony Campolo if he knew why that is.

Tony Campolo

We all lack the fullness of knowledge. First Corinthians 13 says we only know in part, and we only prophesy in part. We look through a glass darkly. We just don't have all the answers. We are struggling for truth; and when someone acts as if he or she has got the whole truth and there is no question about it, that person has reached a level of arrogance that is ungodly.

What we must do as we differ with one another is be humble. We must recognize that we are interpreting the truth as best we can, given that we still have sinful natures that block our apprehension of truth. We are all struggling. We have to recognize that we may be wrong; and instead of fighting with each other, we must listen to each other and ask if there is truth in those who differ from us. I always find that those who hold opposing points of view have more to teach me than people who agree with me!

The life of a Christian isn't meant to be lived outside of community. In fact, Larry Crabb thinks we were created by a relational God to experience relationships with Him and with others that are impossible apart from the gospel.

Larry Crabb

My understanding of connecting is that we literally pour back and forth the energy of Christ—what the Spirit of God puts in us when we're saved. When something comes out of me and goes into you, that is supernatural. Something happens to the soul that can happen in no other way.

I've been a counselor for a long time. But my preoccupation these last couple years has been to look at people with all their struggles and to look at myself with all my struggles and see that these struggles are coming out of disconnected souls. We're not connected to God, to each other, to ourselves.

My theology, my judgment, is that we were designed by a relational God, by a God who is Himself community, to experience a kind of relationship that's impossible apart from the gospel. We want it so bad, but since we've never experienced it the way we want to outside of God, we're not sure it's possible. So we spend our whole lives digging moats around our castles so that nobody gets in and we don't get out. That becomes the fertile soil for all the problems that we have.

> *After reading Larry's classic book* Inside Out, *I reached the somber understanding that some satisfactions will only be experienced when we have our glorified bodies in heaven. Life on earth will always be imperfect, with its incomplete longings and flawed relationships. But after reading Larry's latest book,* Connecting, *I started to see that a glimpse of heaven is still possible for us in the here and now. I asked, "Did Jesus come to give us, at least in part, an example of heaven here on earth?"*

You're right and you're wrong; how's that for clarity? You're right in that we need to define the "unspeakable joy" that Peter speaks of. What does Paul mean in Romans 15 when he says that God has lavished us with joy? What's he talking about there? He's not talking about some independent, good feeling; he's talking about the incredible sense of aliveness that comes when we're in relationship, when we have a passion for Christ and for one another, when there is safety in connecting. The message of *Inside Out* has to spoil the picture a little bit, because we're never going to get it all right until heaven. But we can get some tastes.

My position now—and maybe this is my immaturity speaking; maybe ten years from now I'll look back on this as foolishness—my position is that I'm never going to connect well with many people. I'm finding it more and more my mission and my calling to connect well not only with the Lord but with just a handful of others. You just can't have many friends. You can have a lot of acquaintances, a lot of folks you enjoy, a lot of people you have a great time with, a lot of people that you are nourished by and whom you nourish. But in terms of having relationships that get to the deepest parts of our souls, where the full life of Christ in its richest form in me meets with the same in you—that's really rare, and I don't think we're going to have that kind of connecting on a big scale.

When you sit down on Sunday morning with a couple thousand people, some wonderful things can happen that are fully legitimate and ought to be continued—things like worship and instruction from the Word. But if we call that church, we're making a terrible mistake. That's a preparation for church. Church is a couple of people getting together. That's what Hebrews 10:25 means when it says, "Don't forsake assembling together." The author's not talking about going to a church service on Sunday morning. He's talking about a couple of people being in relationship with God and with each other on the basis of the gospel.

Hebrews 10:24 says, "Think really hard"—the word is *consider* in most translations—"about how to create a fever, how to build a bonfire in one another's souls when you get together." The verse normally is read, "Consider how to stimulate one another to love and good deeds" (NASB). But the literal translation is, "Think about how to create a fever, how to arouse a bonfire, that gets the reality of what God has done into the human soul, and how to flame it up and make it grow large."

What's the Secret?

Church, as Max Lucado put it so well, is a home for every heart. Each of us needs to find our place in God's house of prayer—and open our arms wide to all others who want to come in.

Epilogue

A good book invites us to leave our work-a-day world and come inside where it's cozy and inviting. Opening its pages, we step in through its welcoming front door. We gaze around at the surroundings, check them out, take them in, and make ourselves at home. Later, when it's time to go, we return to our world as if we're returning home from a wonderful vacation. Tired, but refreshed. Happy, but a little sad that it's over.

Let's take some time to unpack our suitcases and remember some of the things we've seen and done. I hope that as you've read, you've felt as if you were pulling up a chair into a small circle of friends. Together we've worshiped God through the telling and hearing of stories about His great love for us. We've been encouraged in our walk with Him. (As you know by now, I emphatically believe that the truthful, open exchange of what we know about Christ is one of the great encouragements of life!) There are many more subjects that could have been addressed within these pages, but I didn't think it was necessary to see and do everything at once. We'll leave those for another day.

Writing the final pages of a book I've been working on for more than two years feels more like writing a benediction than an epilogue. As I consider the lives and the faith of the authors interviewed here, I am reminded of the words of Jesus in John 14:6: "I am the way, the truth, and the life." I believe that in that one, all-encompassing statement, Jesus was saying that He's taught us because He loves us; He can only tell the truth; and life is our reward if we will do this one simple thing: Follow Him. God bless us all.

If you'd like to contact me about what you've read in this book, please e-mail or write me at:

Christopher Coppernoll

P. O. Box 2543

Brentwood, TN 37024

copper@s2sradio.com

Appendix

Here are some excellent ministry organizations you might consider supporting. For the most part, they are humanitarian and evangelical in nature. I've included their Web site addresses in case you'd like to learn more about them online.

American Bible Society
1865 Broadway
New York, NY 10023
www.americanbible.org

The Bible League
16801 Van Dam Road
South Holland, IL 60473
www.gospelcom.net/bibleleague

The Christian Broadcasting Network (CBN)
977 Centerville Turnpike
Virginia Beach, VA 23463
www.cbn.org

Christian Solidarity International (CSI)
870 Hampshire Road, Suite T
Westlake Village, CA 91361
www.csi-int.ch

Compassion International
Colorado Springs, CO 80997
www.compassion.com

Feed the Children
Larry Jones International Ministries, Inc.
P. O. Box 36
Oklahoma City, OK 73101-0036
www.christianity.com/feedthechildren

Focus on the Family
Colorado Springs, CO 80995
www.family.org

Food for the Hungry
7729 East Greenway Road
Scottsdale, AZ 85260
www.fh.org

Mercy Ministries of America
P. O. Box 111060
Nashville, TN 37222-1060
www.mercyministries.org

Prison Fellowship Ministries
P. O. Box 17500
Washington, DC 20041-0500
www.christianity.com/prisonfellowship

Soul2Soul
P. O. Box 2543
Brentwood, TN 37024
www.s2sradio.com

Youth with a Mission
7085 Battlecreek Road SE
Salem, OR 97301
ywam.gospelcom.net

World Vision
P. O. Box 9716, Dept W
Federal Way, WA 98063-9716
www.wvi.org